Lifesaver Lessons™
MATH
GRADE 3

What Are Lifesaver Lessons?

Lifesaver Lessons™ are well-planned, easy-to-implement, curriculum-based lessons. Each lesson contains a complete materials list, step-by-step instructions, a reproducible activity or pattern, and several extension activities.

How Do I Use A Lifesaver Lesson?

Each Lifesaver Lesson™ is designed to decrease your preparation time and increase the amount of quality teaching time with your students. These lessons are great for introducing or reinforcing new concepts. You may want to look through the lessons to see what types of materials to gather. After completing a lesson, be sure to check out the fun-filled extension activities.

What Materials Will I Need?

Most of the materials for each lesson can be easily found in your classroom or school. Check the list of materials below for any items you may need to gather or purchase.

- crayons or colored pencils
- markers
- scissors
- glue
- tape
- rulers
- construction paper
- index cards
- manipulatives
- Froot Loops® cereal
- blank transparencies
- transparency markers
- overhead projector
- sticky-note pads
- candy
- dice
- sentence strips
- paper lunch bags

Project Editor:
Cynthia Holcomb

Writers:
Brenda Dunlap, Cynthia Holcomb, Nicole Iacovazzi,
Kathleen N. Kopp, Mary Ann Lewis, Julie Plowman

Artists:
Jennifer Tipton Bennett, Cathy Spangler Bruce, Clevell Harris,
Susan Hodnett, Mary Lester, Rob Mayworth

Cover Artist:
Jennifer Tipton Bennett

Table Of Contents

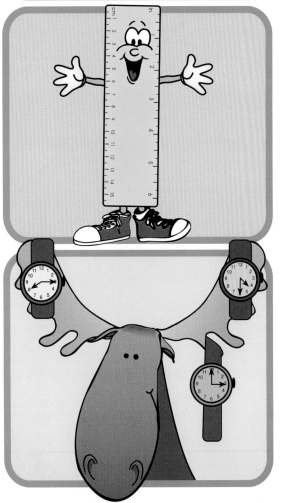

©1997 by THE EDUCATION CENTER, INC.
All rights reserved except as here noted.
ISBN #1-56234-180-4

Manufactured in the United States
10 9 8 7 6 5 4 3 2 1 0

Math Fact Attack

*Your students will be abuzz as they practice
basic math operations.*

Skill: Reviewing addition and subtraction

Estimated Lesson Time: 30 minutes

Teacher Preparation:
Duplicate page 5 for each student.

Materials:
1 copy of page 5 per student

Teacher Reference:
Students can generate math problems
by counting these classroom objects:
• chalkboard erasers
• student chairs
• teacher chairs
• tables
• desks
• computers
• bulletin boards
• light fixtures
• musical instruments
• lunchboxes

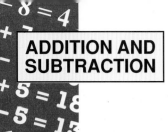

Introducing The Lesson:

Tell students that you became so involved in the book you were reading that you lost track of time and were unable to prepare the math lesson for the day. You know how disappointed the students are, so you will enlist their help in creating a math lesson with information they find in the classroom.

Steps:

1. Ask all students with summer birthdays to stand up. Then ask all students with winter birthdays to raise their hands. Record the number of students in each group on the board, and ask for a volunteer to create a math problem using the information (the numbers of students in both groups could be added together for a total or subtracted to find the difference).

2. Distribute a copy of page 5 to each student. Read the information with your students. Repeat the procedure for finding the information necessary to create the math problems. Then have students solve the problems independently.

3. Challenge students to complete the Bonus Box activity.

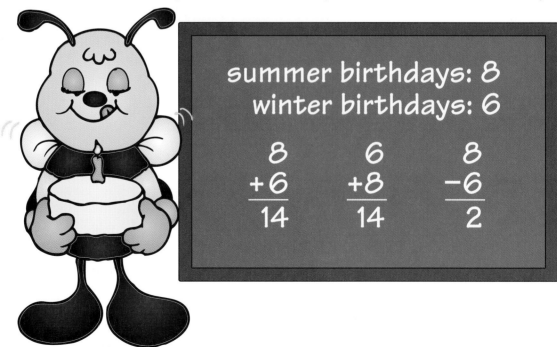

summer birthdays: 8
winter birthdays: 6

$$8 + 6 = 14$$

$$6 + 8 = 14$$

$$8 - 6 = 2$$

Name _____

Math Fact Attack

Find the information needed to create each math problem.
Write the problem in the box.
Then answer each problem.

1. The number of students with blue eyes plus the number of students with brown eyes.

2. The number of buttons worn by the oldest student plus the number of buttons worn by the youngest student.

3. The number of students who brought their lunch plus the number of students who bought their lunch from the cafeteria.

4. The number of students wearing pants minus the number of students wearing dresses.

5. The number of students in the room minus the number of boys in the room.

6. The number of students in the room minus the number of girls in the room.

7. The number of flags in the room plus the number of fingers the teacher is holding up.

8. The number of doors in the room plus your age.

9. The number of trash cans in the room minus the number of pencil sharpeners.

10. The number of problems on this paper minus the number of teachers in the room.

| 1. |
| 2. |
| 3. |
| 4. |
| 5. |
| 6. |
| 7. |
| 8. |
| 9. |
| 10. |

Bonus Box: Write a math problem on the back of this paper. Use information about the classroom in the problem.

How To Extend The Lesson:

- Have students check their answers on the reproducible by demonstrating the information in each problem. Have students stand up to represent the numbers requested in the student-related problems. Have them draw diagrams to show problems that require objects in the room.

- Have students take a survey of another classroom and class to find the information requested on the reproducible. Have them complete the reproducible again with the new information.

- Ask students to try using a different operation to solve each problem on the reproducible. Discuss which problems can be worked and which ones can't be done.

- Distribute a copy of the pattern below to each student. Instruct the student to assemble the pattern to form a number cube. Place students in pairs. Each student rolls her number cube. The pair creates as many math problems as possible using the numbers they have rolled.

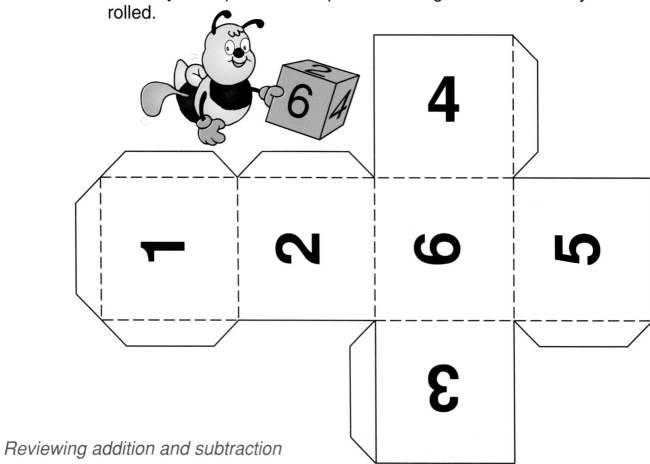

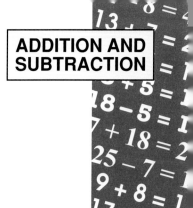

Regrouping Rally

Help students reach the winner's circle as they use regrouping to find the sums.

Skill: Regrouping with 2-digit addition

Estimated Lesson Time: 45 minutes

Teacher Preparation:
1. Duplicate the reproducible on page 9 for each student.
2. Gather the supplies listed below.

Materials:
1 copy of page 9 per student
classroom set of Cuisenaire® Rods (or use the patterns provided on page 91)
1 die for each pair of students
1 blue and 1 red crayon per student

Quick Tip:
Help your students create straight columns while working on math problems with this easy tip. Instruct students to turn a sheet of lined notebook paper sideways and use the lines as column dividers. The lines help students keep each numeral in its correct place!

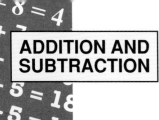

Introducing The Lesson:

Ask your students if they have seen or heard of a rally. Explain that a rally is a long-distance car race. Tell students that as a warm-up for a regrouping rally, they will play a game to practice regrouping ones into tens. Remind students that when they add numbers in a column, the numbers must be regrouped to the next place value when the sum reaches ten or more.

Steps:

1. Place students in pairs. Give each pair 20 unit cubes, 20 tens rods, 1 hundred square, and 1 die.

2. Have each partner take turns rolling the die. The student counts out an amount of unit cubes as indicated on the die. When he gets ten or more cubes, he must trade for a tens rod. The first player to trade tens rods for a hundred square is the winner.

3. After several rounds of play, distribute a copy of page 9 to each student.

4. Allow time for each student to complete the reproducible. Then challenge students to complete the Bonus Box activity.

I have 13 cubes. I can trade in 10 of the cubes for a tens rod.

Name_____

Regrouping Rally

Add to find the sums.
You will have to regroup to solve some of the problems.

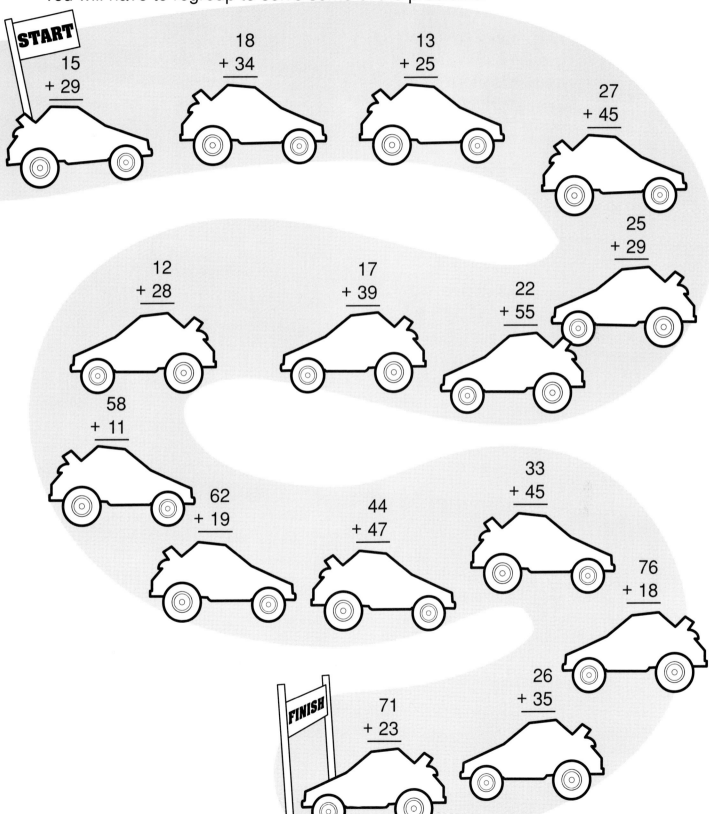

START
```
  15
+ 29
```

```
  18
+ 34
```

```
  13
+ 25
```

```
  27
+ 45
```

```
  25
+ 29
```

```
  12
+ 28
```

```
  17
+ 39
```

```
  22
+ 55
```

```
  58
+ 11
```

```
  62
+ 19
```

```
  44
+ 47
```

```
  33
+ 45
```

```
  76
+ 18
```

```
  26
+ 35
```

FINISH
```
  71
+ 23
```

Bonus Box: If you had to regroup, color the car's wheels red. If you did not regroup, color the car's wheels blue.

⑨

©1997 The Education Center, Inc. • *Lifesaver Lessons*™ • Grade 3 • TEC505 • Key p. 95

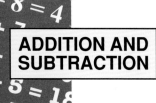

How To Extend The Lesson:

• Ask each student to create one addition problem that requires regrouping and one that does not need regrouping. Collect the problems and write them on an overhead transparency. Have the students try to identify which problems will need to be regrouped before they actually solve the problems.

• Prepare an easy-to-update center activity that will reinforce regrouping practice. Program a strip of tagboard with a list of ten numbers; then laminate for durability. Post the list in a center. Use a wipe-off marker to write an operation (such as +14) at the top of the list. Instruct each student to copy the ten math problems on a sheet of paper and solve them. The next day, wipe off the old operation and replace it with a new one. The center will have ten new problems to solve!

• Practice regrouping with an activity that will keep students on the move. Have each student write a two-digit number on a self-stick note and attach it to her shirt. Instruct each student to carry a pencil and paper with her as you place the students in two lines, facing each other. At your signal, the two students facing each other write and solve an addition problem using the numbers on their self-stick notes. Then have the students in each line rotate one position. Repeat the procedure until a desired number of problems have been solved.

• Have each student create a word problem that will require regrouping to solve. Ask for student volunteers to write their problems on the board for their classmates to solve. For an added challenge, have students include unnecessary information in their word problems.

Sally had 39 pennies. Her sister gave her 42 more pennies and 15 nickels. How many pennies does Sally have now?

Jerry has 14 rabbits and 16 birds. He feeds his pets twice a day. How many pets does he own?

Subtraction Snack Shack

Send your little piggies to market for a shopping spree that reinforces the concept of regrouping.

Skill: Regrouping with 2-digit subtraction

Estimated Lesson Time: 45 minutes

Teacher Preparation:

1. Duplicate page 13 for each student.
2. Gather the materials listed below.
3. Write "90¢" on the chalkboard.

Materials:

1 copy of page 13 per student

class set of index cards, each programmed with a coin value ranging from 5¢ to 29¢ (The number in the ones place of each number should be five or larger.)

Teacher Reference:

Use the term *regrouping* with your students instead of "borrowing" or "trading." The term *regrouping* is used in both addition and subtraction, and the student will have a better understanding of the concept if the same term is used when discussing either operation.

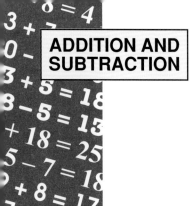

Introducing The Lesson:

Tell students that they are going to participate in a little spending spree. Write the amount "90¢" on the chalkboard, and distribute to each student an index card programmed with a coin value. Have each student in turn come to the board and subtract the amount written on his card from the total value. When the total reaches zero, or if it becomes too low to subtract from, begin again with 90¢ and continue until each student has had a turn.

Steps:

1. As each student subtracts his coin amount, discuss the rules for regrouping.

2. After each student has had a turn, distribute a copy of page 13 to each student.

3. Provide time for students to complete the reproducible.

4. Challenge students to complete the Bonus Box activity.

Name_____

Subtraction Snack Shack

Use the picture to help solve each problem.
Show your work in each box.

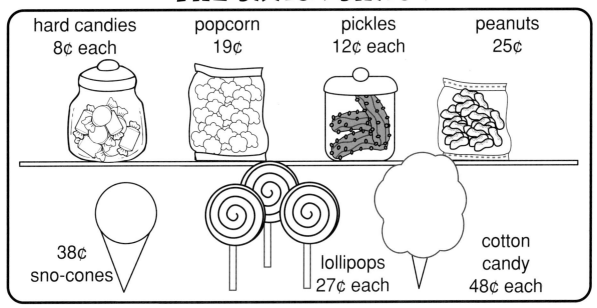

THE SNACK SHACK

hard candies
8¢ each

popcorn
19¢

pickles
12¢ each

peanuts
25¢

38¢
sno-cones

lollipops
27¢ each

cotton
candy
48¢ each

Joe's Snack Attack

Joe has 90¢.
He bought a sno-cone.
How much money is left?

Then Joe bought some peanuts.
How much money is left?

Joe also bought popcorn.
How much money is left?

What could Joe buy with the money left over?

_____

Jane's Snack Attack

Jane has 90¢.
She bought cotton candy.
How much money is left?

Then Jane bought a lollipop.
How much money is left?

Jane also bought a pickle.
How much money is left?

What could Jane buy with the money left over?

_____

Bonus Box: What would you buy from the Snack Shack with 90¢? Make a list on the back of this paper.

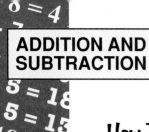

How To Extend The Lesson:

- Bring a jar of pennies to class. Instruct each student to take two pennies from the jar and write down the date from each penny. Have the student subtract the last two digits of the older date from the last two digits of the newer date. Then have the student return the pennies to the jar and repeat the procedure until he has created ten problems.

- Play a version of Hangman using subtraction problems. Write a subtraction problem that requires regrouping on the board. Ask a student volunteer to come to the board to solve the problem. If the student solves the problem correctly, write a tally mark on the board. If the student answers incorrectly, draw a part of the hangman on the board. Challenge the class to earn ten tally marks before you complete the hangman drawing.

- Distribute a supply of plastic coins (or use the coin patterns on page 92) so that each student has an amount less than $1.00. Place each student with a partner and have the pair determine the value of each partner's coins. Then instruct each pair to write and solve a subtraction problem using the two coin amounts. Have students switch partners and repeat the process until a determined number of problems have been written and solved.

- Duplicate a supply of the patterns below to create subtraction problems for a math center activity. Program the patterns with subtraction problems that require regrouping, as well as with problems where regrouping is not required. Program the back of each pattern for self-checking.

Regrouping with 2-digit subtraction

The Dice Drop

This fast-paced activity will have your students rolling towards success with multiplication!

Skill: Practicing multiplication facts through 6

Estimated Lesson Time: 30 minutes

Teacher Preparation:
1. Duplicate the reproducible on page 17 for each student.
2. Gather the materials listed below.

Materials:
1 copy of page 17 per student
2 dice per student pair (a die pattern is provided on page 6)

Teacher Reference:
Review the following terminology with your students:

Equation: An equation is a sentence that shows that two different numbers or mathematical expressions are equal to each other. An equation uses the equals sign (=), such as in the statement 3 x 4 **=** 12.

Factor: A factor is a number that is being multiplied. In the equation above, the factors are **3** and **4**.

Multiplication: Multiplication is one of the four basic operations of arithmetic. Multiplication allows you to add the same number a specified number of times. The equation 3 x 4 can also be solved by adding 3 + 3 + 3 + 3, or adding 4 + 4 + 4.

Product: A product is the result of two factors being multiplied. In the equation 3 x 4 = 12, the product is **12**.

Times: Times is another way of saying "multiplied by." The above equation can be read "Three multiplied by four equals twelve," *or* "Three times four equals twelve."

Introducing The Lesson:

Tell students that they are going to work in pairs to roll their way through multiplication practice. Review the terminology on page 15 with your students. Then explain that each pair of students will use two dice to create and solve a set of multiplication problems.

Steps:

1. Distribute a copy of page 17 to each student. Review the directions and demonstrate how to create a problem with a roll of the dice.

2. Place students in pairs to complete the reproducible. Distribute a pair of dice to each set of partners.

3. Each partner will take turns rolling the dice to determine the factors for each multiplication problem. Each partner records the factors on her reproducible, writes a multiplication sentence with the factors, and then finds the product.

4. Provide time for each pair to create ten equations.

5. Challenge students to complete the Bonus Box activity.

The Dice Drop

Taking turns with your partner, roll the dice five times each.
After each roll, record the numbers shown on the dice as factors.
Write a multiplication sentence with the factors.
Then find the product of the sentence.

Roll Number	Factors	Multiplication Sentence	Product

Bonus Box: Add the products above for a total score. Compare your total with another set of partners.

17

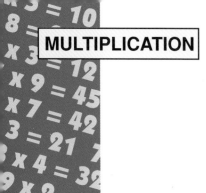

How To Extend The Lesson:

- Arrange students in small groups. Have each group member roll two dice, multiply the numbers together, and then record the product on a sheet of paper. After each group member has had a turn, instruct the members to use the products for these activities:
  —Arrange the products in order from least to greatest.
  —Determine which products are even numbers and which are odd numbers.
  —Find the product with the largest number in the tens place and the product with the largest number in the ones place.
  —Add the products together. Compare to see which group had the largest (or smallest) sum.

- Distribute an index card to each student. Instruct each student to write a numeral from one to six on the card. Call two students to come to the front of the room and show their cards to the class. The first student to say the product of the two numbers earns a point. Play until a student earns five points, or until every student has had the opportunity to earn a point.

- Prepare a bar graph as shown below. Have each student roll two dice and multiply the numbers. Then have her record each product on the appropriate place on the graph.

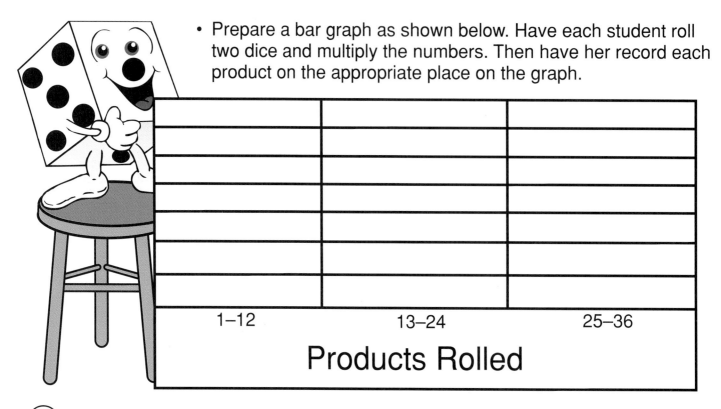

1–12	13–24	25–36

Products Rolled

Card Sharks

Multiplication success is in the cards with this fact-reinforcement game!

Skill: Practicing multiplication facts through 10

Estimated Lesson Time: 30 minutes

Teacher Preparation:
1. Duplicate a copy of page 21 for each student.
2. Provide each student with ten index cards or ten 3" x 4" tagboard strips.

Materials:
1 copy of page 21 per student
10 index cards or tagboard
   strips per student
crayons

Quick Tip:
This game can also be played using decks of playing cards instead of programmed index cards. Use a deck of cards for every four students. Give each student one suit of cards. Assign the ace a value of one, and each face card a value of ten. Then have students play the game as described on page 20.

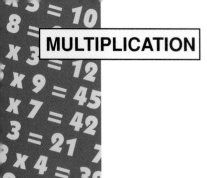

Introducing The Lesson:

Tell students that this math lesson will be a great deal of fun as they work in pairs to play a multiplication card game. Explain that each student will need to follow your directions to create a set of cards to use in the game.

Steps:

1. Distribute ten index cards and a copy of page 21 to each student.

2. Instruct each student to write one numeral from 1 to 10 on each index card.

3. Pair students together to complete the reproducible. To begin, each student places his cards facedown in a stack. Have each partner flip over his top card. The partners use the two numbers as factors for a multiplication problem, which they will write and solve on the reproducible.

4. Have students repeat the steps to create ten problems.

5. Challenge students to complete the Bonus Box activity.

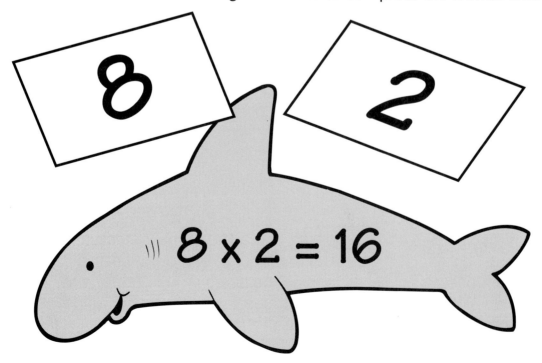

Name_____

Card Sharks

Follow your teacher's directions to make a set of cards and create ten different
  multiplication problems.
Write and solve each problem on a shark.
Then use the color code to complete the page.

1.

6.

2.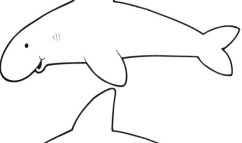

7.

3.

8.

4.

9.

5.

10.

Color the sharks' fins using the following code:
   Green   — even-numbered products
   Yellow   — odd-numbered products
   Red dots   — the shark with the greatest product
   Blue dots — the shark with the least product

Bonus Box: On another sheet of paper, write the products in order from least to greatest.

How To Extend The Lesson:

• Pair students for a game similar to War using their programmed index cards. The partners sit facing each other with their cards facedown in front of them. On the count of three, each student turns over the top card of his stack and places it in the space between the players. The first student to correctly identify the product of the two numbers wins the round and puts both cards in his stack. Play continues until one student wins all the cards, or until a designated time period is called and students count to see who has collected the most cards.

• Get students moving with a musical-chairs type of activity to practice multiplication facts. To prepare, write a number from one to ten on the board. Instruct each student to select one of her programmed index cards and place it on her desk. At your signal, each student takes a sheet of paper and a pencil and moves to the desk in front of her. The student copies the number from the card on the desk and the number on the board as factors on her paper, then solves the equation. After finding the product, the student waits for your signal to move to the next desk. Continue the procedure until each student has traveled to every desk.

• Use copies of the shark pattern below to program multiplication problems for a learning center activity, or for students to use as flash cards for independent practice.

Playful Pups

Students use problem-solving skills to sort these playful pups by a variety of attributes.

Skill: Sorting

Estimated Lesson Time: 30 minutes

Teacher Preparation:
1. Duplicate page 25 for each student.
2. Gather the materials below.

Materials:
1 copy of page 25 per student
crayons
scissors

Teacher Reference:
Attributes For Creating Student Groups:
- gender
- color of hair
- color of eyes
- number of letters in the student's first name
- number of siblings
- favorite subjects
- age
- types of pets
- transportation to school
- lunch choice

Introducing The Lesson:

Tell the class that they are going to look at different ways to sort things into groups. Ask seven or eight student volunteers to come to the front of the room. Write the word "students" on the board. Explain to the class that the subject of this group is *students,* but if they look closely enough, the class should be able to find a way to divide this group into two smaller categories. Have the seated students observe the group and suggest several ways to divide them into two categories. Possibilities include long-sleeved shirts and short-sleeved shirts, or pants and skirts. Write the names of the two categories under the word "students" on the board. Then challenge students to divide each category into two smaller headings. Record these headings under the appropriate category (see the example below).

Steps:

1. Tell students that each of them will be working with a partner to group a collection of playful puppies.

2. Distribute crayons, scissors, and a copy of page 25 to each student.

3. Pair each student with a partner.

4. Provide time for students to color and cut out the puppies on the reproducible, then complete the sorting activity.

5. Challenge students to complete the Bonus Box activity.

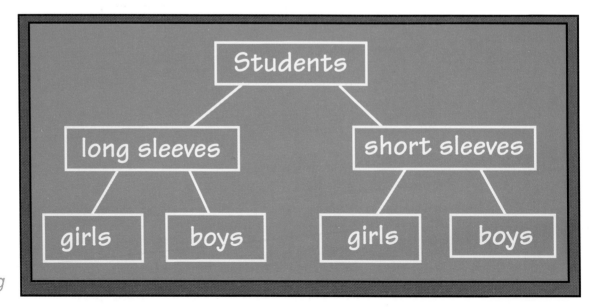

Playful Pups

Color the puppy in each box.
Cut the boxes apart.
Use the puppies in a sorting activity with a partner.

Put both sets of puppy pictures together.
Sort the puppies into two groups. Name these groups.
Then divide each group into two smaller sections. Name each section.
Record the information on the Sort Report.

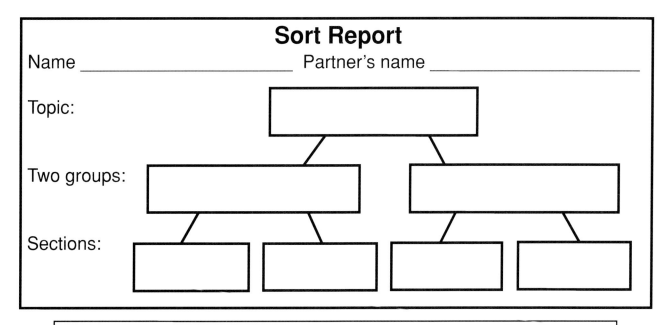

Bonus Box: Put all the puppies together. Sort the puppies in a different way. Record the new information on the back of the Sort Report.

How To Extend The Lesson:

• Have students express the fractional amount of puppies in each section. Remind students that the denominator of each fraction should be 12, since there are 12 puppies altogether.

• Have each pair of students arrange the puppy pictures in a bar graph format according to the number of colors on each puppy. Provide a blank bar graph on which students can transfer the information from picture form to recorded data.

• Place students in groups (four or five per group). Have each group decide on a way to sort themselves into two smaller groups, then sort each of these groups into two smaller sections. Have each group stand in front of the class in their sorted arrangement while the class determines the methods of grouping.

• Ask students to bring in spare buttons from home. Store the buttons in a jar and place the jar in a learning center with copies of the Sort Report. A student visits the center, determines a method for sorting the buttons, and records the results on a Sort Report.

• Instruct each pair of students to use two sections as attributes for a Venn diagram. Give each pair two lengths of yarn to fashion into circles for the diagram. Have the students place each puppy picture in the appropriate area of the diagram.

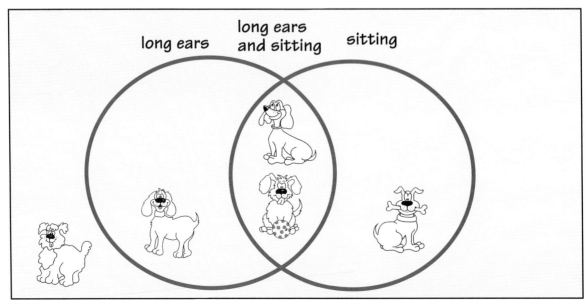

Made To Order

Students put problem-solving and money skills to work as they order from a catalog of toys galore.

Skill: Solving money problems

Estimated Lesson Time: 30 minutes

Teacher Preparation:
1. Duplicate a copy of page 29 for each student.
2. Duplicate a copy of the dollar bills on page 28 for each student.

Materials:
1 copy of page 29 per student
1 copy of the bills on page 28 per student

Teacher Reference:

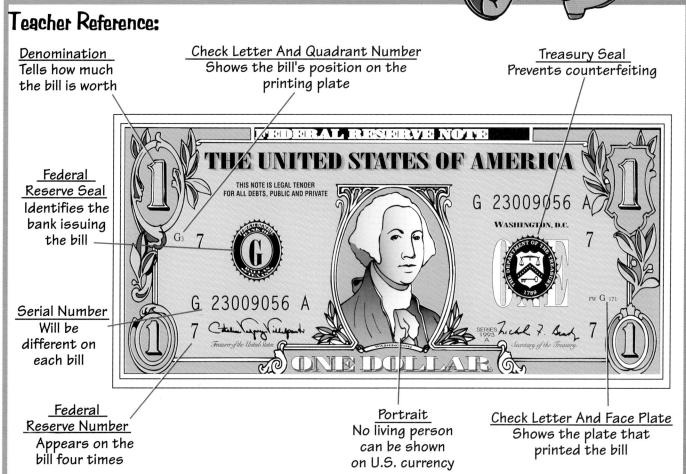

Denomination
Tells how much the bill is worth

Check Letter And Quadrant Number
Shows the bill's position on the printing plate

Treasury Seal
Prevents counterfeiting

Federal Reserve Seal
Identifies the bank issuing the bill

Serial Number
Will be different on each bill

Federal Reserve Number
Appears on the bill four times

Portrait
No living person can be shown on U.S. currency

Check Letter And Face Plate
Shows the plate that printed the bill

Introducing The Lesson:

Distribute a copy of the bills below to each student. Point out the features of the bills as labeled on page 27. Then tell students that they will "spend" some money as they do a little imaginary shopping from a catalog ad.

Steps:

1. Distribute a copy of page 29 to each student.

2. Allow time for students to list and total purchases within their $10.00 limit (or whatever limit you designate).

3. Challenge students to complete the Bonus Box activity.

Money has been called bread, dough, bucks, clams, moolah, loot, simoleans, and greenbacks!

Made To Order

Place an order from this catalog.
Your teacher will tell you how much money you may spend.
Fill in the order form.
Add to find the total.

Amount of money you may spend: _____

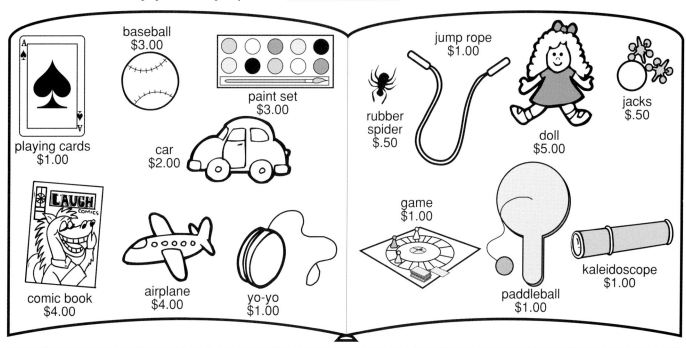

Order Form

Name of item:	Cost:
Total:	

Bonus Box: Trade papers with a classmate. Check each other's work.

How To Extend The Lesson:

• Collect sale advertisements from newspapers or mail-order catalogs. Have students look through the materials to create a wish list with a pre-determined amount of money to "spend."

• Tie in some money-related literature with *Alexander Who Used To Be Rich Last Sunday* by Judith Viorst (Simon and Schuster Children's Books, 1987). Despite good intentions, Alexander's attempts to save money just never seem to work out. After reading the story, give each youngster a dollar's worth of imitation coins as follows: seven dimes, four nickels, and ten pennies. Reread the story—having students set aside coins as Alexander spends his money. Each time money is spent, have students determine how much money Alexander has left before you continue the story.

• *If You Made A Million* by David Schwartz (Morrow Junior Books, 1994) introduces students to the world of banks, interest, checks, and loans. After reading the story, give each student several copies of the check pattern below. Have the student practice writing checks to several of his classmates. (If desired, assign students the names of classmates to write checks to so that each student receives an equal amount.) Collect and distribute the checks to the designated students; then have each student add up the total of his checks.

```
_____
_____                                          _____ 19____   28-8790/2869
_____

                                                              ┌──────────────┐
Pay To The Order Of _____ $│              │
                                                              └──────────────┘

                         _____ Dollars

       The Best Bank
       Sunshine, VA _____
          00020

       3827344990: 034 876 323 7447
```

©1997 The Education Center, Inc. • *Lifesaver Lessons*™ • Grade 3 • TEC505

Rock 'n' Roll

Students won't miss a beat as they roll through this partner activity to generate word problems.

Skill: Writing word problems

Estimated Lesson Time: 30 minutes

Teacher Preparation:
1. Duplicate the reproducible on page 33 for each pair of students.
2. Collect two small pebble-sized rocks for each pair of students.

Materials:
1 copy of page 33 per pair of students
2 small rocks per pair of students
1 sheet of 8 1/2" x 11" paper per pair of students

Teacher Reference:
Remind students of some key words for each math operation.

Addition	**Subtraction**	**Multiplication**	**Division**
plus	minus	multiply	divide
all together	subtract	times	for each
add	take away	each	
in all	are left		

Introducing The Lesson:

Tell students that they are going to work in pairs to write and solve word problems. Addition, subtraction, multiplication, or division can be used in this activity.

Steps:

1. Divide students into pairs.

2. Distribute a copy of the Rock 'n' Roll gameboard (page 33) to each pair.

3. Also distribute a piece of paper and two small rocks to each pair.

4. Instruct each pair to follow the directions on the reproducible.

5. Have pairs repeat this procedure until five word problems have been written on their papers.

6. Challenge pairs to complete the Bonus Box activity.

Rock 'n' Roll

Roll your two rocks onto the gameboard.
On the paper, record the two numerals on which they've landed.
Use those two numerals to write a word problem.
Include the answer to the word problem on the back of your paper.

6	8	9	7
4	3	1	5
7	6	8	2
5	0	4	10
2	9	1	3

Bonus Box: Draw a picture that makes sense for each word problem you have written.

How To Extend The Lesson:

• Increase the difficulty level of the activity. Have students repro-gram the Rock 'n' Roll gameboard with two- and three-digit numbers and play the game again.

• Give each student a copy of the form below on which to write and illustrate a word problem. Ask him to include the answer on the back of the paper. Collect all the word problems and compile them into a class book titled "Rock 'n' Roll Math."

• Divide students into small groups and have groups develop their own word-problem games. Have each group design a gameboard, write a set of instructions, provide or make needed game components, and demonstrate the game to the class. Store the completed games in a math center.

word problem written by:

Batter Up!

Have students step up to the plate to choose the operation for these grand-slam baseball problems.

Skill: Choosing the operation

Estimated Lesson Time: 40 minutes

Teacher Preparation:

1. Duplicate the reproducible on page 37 for each student.
2. Program six sentence strips as shown below. Fold each strip at the far right edge to hide the operation symbol.

Materials:
1 copy of page 37 per student
6 programmed sentence strips

in all	
altogether	+
total	+

how many more ... than	—
how many are left?	—
difference	

Choosing the operation (35)

Introducing The Lesson:

Ask your students to volunteer some information about the game of base-ball. Record each statement on the board. After a desired number of statements have been recorded, tell students that they will refer to the information to compose addition or subtraction word problems using the information.

Steps:

1. Use the programmed sentence strips to reinforce key words to look for when determining the operations needed for solving word problems. Show each folded strip to the class and have them determine which operation should be used with each term. Confirm the answer by unfolding the end of the strip to reveal the operation symbol.

2. Challenge each student to compose an addition or a subtraction word problem using information written on the board.

3. Ask student volunteers to share their problems with the class. After each volunteer reads his problem, ask the class to determine which operation is needed to solve the problem.

4. Distribute a copy of page 37 to each student. Provide time for each student to complete the reproducible.

5. Challenge students to complete the Bonus Box activity.

A baseball game has nine innings.
If a batter makes three strikes during his turn at bat, he strikes out.
There are nine field positions.
A baseball is about nine inches around.
A baseball weighs about five ounces.
Regulation bats can't be longer than 42 inches.
There are four bases on the field.
Each base is 90 feet apart.
If a pitcher throws four balls out of the strike zone to a batter, the
  batter gets to walk to first base.
There are three outs per inning.
A "perfect" game is 27 batters up, 27 batters down—no one makes a hit or gets on base.

Batter Up!

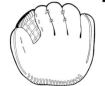

Read each problem.
Decide which operation to use.
Then solve the problem.

	✓ I need to		Answer
	Add	Subtract	
1.			
2.			
3.			
4.			
5.			
6.			
7.			
8.			

1. Myron made 4 hits in the first inning, 2 hits in the second inning, and 2 hits in the fourth inning. How many hits did he make in all?

2. There were 9 batters in the bottom of the third inning. Four batters hit foul balls. How many players did not hit foul balls?

3. In one inning, Pete threw 5 fastballs, 4 curveballs, 7 sliders, and 3 knuckleballs. How many pitches did he throw in all?

4. The Giants scored 11 runs during the game. The Red Sox scored 14 runs. How many runs were scored altogether?

5. Bruno had two hits. The first ball traveled 84 feet, and the second ball traveled 79 feet. How many more feet did the first ball travel?

6. A baseball game has 9 innings. So far, 5 innings of a game have been played. How many innings are left to play?

7. The Springfield Sluggers must travel 35 miles to get to Norris Stadium. They must travel 67 miles to get to Rogers Field. How much further do they travel when they play at Rogers Field than at Norris Stadium?

8. During the game, Chavez scored 4 runs, Miller scored 6 runs, and Wilson scored 3 runs. How many total runs did the three players score?

Bonus Box: Lou Gehrig played in 2,130 baseball games without ever missing a game. Find out another fact about a famous baseball player.

How To Extend The Lesson:

• Program an index card for each pair of students with the name of a sport. Have each pair research the sport for statistics and information. Then instruct each pair to write five word problems using the information. Compile the questions into reproducible practice sheets for the class to complete.

• Use a topic of class study for creating word problems. Challenge students to use information from social studies, science, or health lessons to compose several word problems. Provide time during the appropriate subject for students to share their word problems with the class.

• Have students take their places at bat as they select the correct operation for solving word problems. Duplicate a copy of the pattern below for each student. Instruct each student to write an addition sign on one side of the bat and a subtraction sign on the other side. Read several word problems to the class. Have each student hold up her bat to show which operation is needed to solve each problem.

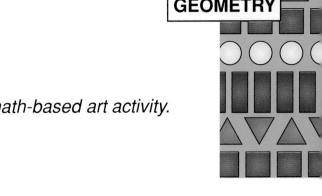

Shape Up!

Reinforce basic geometric shapes with this math-based art activity.

Skill: Identifying geometric shapes

Estimated Lesson Time: 30 minutes

Teacher Preparation:
Duplicate page 41 for each student.

Materials:
1 copy of page 41 per student
crayons (optional)

Teacher Reference:

A *circle* is a round, closed figure with all its boundary points the same distance from the center.

An *ellipse* is a closed, oval, plane figure that is not as round as a circle.

A *rectangle* is a plane figure with four straight sides that form right angles.

A *rhombus* is a plane figure with four straight sides of the same length that do not form right angles.

A *square* is a rectangle with four straight sides of equal length that form four right angles.

A *triangle* is a plane figure with three straight sides.

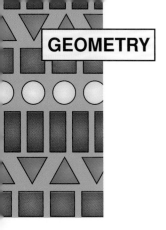

Introducing The Lesson:

Look around the classroom for a few seconds; then announce to your students that you need to get the classroom into shape—or more accurately, shapes. Write the word *circle* on the board. Ask students to name objects in the classroom that are circular in shape. Record their responses on the board.

Steps:

1. Repeat the above procedure to have students name classroom objects that are square, rectangular, and triangular.

2. Challenge students to use these geometric shapes to create pictures.

3. Distribute a copy of page 41 to each student.

4. Provide time for students to draw pictures according to the instructions on the page. If time allows, have students color their drawings.

5. Challenge students to complete the Bonus Box activity.

circle	square	rectangle	triangle
clock	window	paper	shelf
wheel	floor tile	notebook	prism
globe	picture	door	
ball	intercom	computer	
orange			

Name _____

Shape Up!

Follow the instructions to create a shape picture in each box.

1. Draw a tree.
   Use a rectangle and a circle.

4. Draw a robot.
   List the shapes you used.

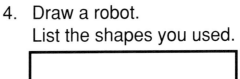

2. Draw a house.
   Use a triangle, a square,
   and four rectangles.

5. Draw a rocket.
   List the shapes you used.

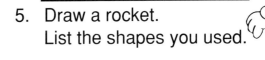

3. Draw a cat.
   List the shapes you used.

6. Draw a truck.
   List the shapes you used.

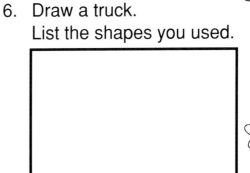

Bonus Box: For each shape, list five objects in your house having that shape.

©1997 The Education Center, Inc. • *Lifesaver Lessons*™ • Grade 3 • TEC505

41

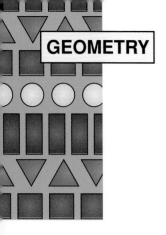

How To Extend The Lesson:

- Enlist the help of your students in creating a collection of objects that represent solid and flat geometric shapes. Place the items—which might include an empty cereal box, a paper-towel roll, an eraser, a pencil, a book, a party hat, a tennis ball, and a box of tissues—in a large box. Invite your students to examine each item and identify it by shape name.

- Have a Shapely Snack Celebration. Encourage students to bring in a supply of snack foods in various geometric shapes. Arrange the snacks on paper plates. Announce the name of a shape; then have each student select one item of that shape. Continue in this manner until all snacks have been taken. Then invite students to munch the tasty shapes.

- Put your class on the lookout for shapes with a mini field trip. Walk around the school grounds and have students find examples of shapes used in floor tiles, brick walls, ceiling tiles, windows, intercoms, and other construction features. Challenge each student to keep a tally-mark record of the different shapes he observes.

- Create abstract works of art by having students cut geometric shapes from wallpaper samples, wrapping paper, or fabric scraps. Instruct each student to arrange and then glue his shapes on a sheet of construction paper. Display the finished projects on a bulletin board with the title "We're Getting Into Shapes!"

Scrambled Numbers

Reinforce place value and number sense with this "egg-citing" lesson!

Skill: Determining place value to the thousands

Estimated Lesson Time: 30 minutes

Teacher Preparation:
1. Duplicate a copy of page 45 for each student.
2. Program an index card with a numeral from 0 to 9 for each student.

Materials:
1 copy of page 45 per student
1 programmed index card per student

Teacher Reference:
Reinforce the concept of place value by having students determine if the following items would number in the ones, tens, hundreds, or thousands:

- names in the phone book
- toothpicks in a box
- pieces of popcorn in a bowl
- students in a classroom
- items on a fast-food menu
- different types of cookies in the grocery store
- hairs on a person's head
- bananas in a bunch
- keys on a computer
- pieces of bubble gum in a pack
- books in the library
- letters in a first name
- fish in an aquarium

Determining place value to the thousands

Introducing The Lesson:

Tell students that they are going to work together to scramble numbers into different place values. Distribute a programmed index card to each student. Inform each student that the numeral on her card may take on the value of ones, tens, hundreds, or thousands.

Steps:

1. Call four students to come to the front of the room with their index cards. Instruct them to hold their cards in front of them so that the class can observe each numeral.

2. Ask a student volunteer to arrange the students so that their numerals make the largest (or smallest) possible number.

3. Ask another volunteer to rearrange the students so that the largest (or smallest) numeral is in the hundreds (or tens) place.

4. Continue calling groups of four to the front of the room and asking volunteers to arrange them in designated numbers until all students have had a chance to participate.

5. Distribute a copy of page 45 to each student. Provide time for students to complete the reproducible.

6. Challenge students to complete the Bonus Box activity.

Scrambled Numbers

Follow the directions to create numbers for each group of numerals.

4, 3, 6, 2

Write the largest number. _____

Write the smallest number. _____

Write a number with the smallest numeral in the tens place. _____

Write a number with the largest numeral in the hundreds place. _____

2, 9, 0, 6

Write the largest number. _____

Write the smallest number. _____

Write a number with the smallest numeral in the tens place. _____

Write a number with the largest numeral in the hundreds place. _____

7, 8, 1, 5

Write the largest number. _____

Write the smallest number. _____

Write a number with the smallest numeral in the tens place. _____

Write a number with the largest numeral in the hundreds place. _____

3, 0, 8, 4

Write the largest number. _____

Write the smallest number. _____

Write a number with the smallest numeral in the tens place. _____

Write a number with the largest numeral in the hundreds place. _____

2, 5, 1, 7

Write the largest number. _____

Write the smallest number. _____

Write a number with the smallest numeral in the tens place. _____

Write a number with the largest numeral in the hundreds place. _____

Bonus Box: Arrange the numbers you created with each set in order from least to greatest.

(45)

©1997 The Education Center, Inc. • *Lifesaver Lessons*™ • Grade 3 • TEC505 • Key p. 95

How To Extend The Lesson:

- Place students in groups of four. Give each group a die (or use copies of the die pattern on page 6). Instruct each student to roll the die four times and record the first roll as a numeral in the ones place, the second roll as a numeral in the tens place, the third roll as a numeral in the hundreds place, and the fourth roll as a numeral in the thousands place. After each group member has had a turn, have each member compare to see who rolled the highest number.

- Instruct each student to think of a four-digit number. Have the student use place-value blocks (or copies of the place-value patterns on page 91) to create a model of the number he selected. Then have the class arrange the models in order from least to greatest.

- Challenge students to collect 1,000 objects. Decide on an easy-to-count item to collect, such as soft-drink caps, pennies, or milk-jug lids. Designate a box in your room as the collection site. Provide time each week for a student to count the items in the box and place them in groups of ten. Secure each group of ten in a sandwich-size resealable bag. When ten sandwich-size bags have been filled, place them in a gallon-size bag. When ten gallon-size bags have been filled, your students have reached their goal!

- Have each student write down the last four digits of his phone number. Have students work in small groups to determine who has the largest numeral in each position. Then have the group members determine who has the largest and the smallest four-digit number.

- Reward students for their hard work in determining place value with copies of the award tokens.

Determining place value to the thousands

10, 100, 10
hun
1, .01, .001,
thousands,
1000, 10,00
thousandth
001, .0001,
nes, tens,

Number Roundup

Reinforce the concept of rounding numbers with this rootin'-tootin' activity.

Skill: Rounding numbers to the thousands place

Estimated Lesson Time: 30 minutes

Teacher Preparation:
1. Duplicate a copy of page 49 for each student.
2. Program a set of 20 index cards with numbers to be used for rounding. (See the examples on page 48.)

Materials:
1 copy of page 49 per student
a set of programmed index cards
20 index cards per student pair

Teacher Reference:
Remind students how to round numbers with these three steps:

Step 1: Find the place value of the numeral to be rounded.   <u>4</u>,902

Step 2: Look at the digit to its right.   <u>4</u>,902
   If the digit is less than five, round the numeral down.   ↑
   If the digit is five or greater, round the numeral up.

Step 3: Change each digit to the right of the rounded numeral to zero.
     <u>5</u>,000

Rounding numbers to the thousands place (47)

0, 100, 100

nths

.01, .001, .

housands, te

000, 10,000

housandths.

01, .0001, .0

nes, tens, l

7,350

1,099

9,502

3,499

2,813

6,423

5,912

6,794

4,533

8,615

2,499

3,523

9,190

5,375

1,642

4,871

9,090

1,858

7,329

8,119

Introducing The Lesson:

Tell students that they are going to participate in a Number Roundup, where some numbers actually *are* rounded up—and some are rounded down! After a practice session with the class, students will work in pairs to conduct their own partner roundup.

Steps:

1. Explain the rules for the roundup by reviewing the steps for rounding numbers on page 47.

2. Use the programmed index cards as flash cards for the class to use to practice rounding.

3. Place students in pairs. Give 20 index cards to each pair. Instruct the students to program the cards to match your set.

4. Distribute a copy of page 49 to each student. Explain the directions for completing the reproducible as follows:

   • Shuffle the index cards and place them facedown in a stack.
   • Each partner starts with ten points.
   • Each partner takes a turn drawing a card and rounding the number to the thousands place. He records the number on the reproducible. If he rounds the number up, he adds one point to his score. If he rounds the number down, he subtracts a point from his score.
   • Play continues until all cards have been used. The winner is the player with the highest score at the end of the roundup.

5. After students have finished the roundup, challenge them to complete the Bonus Box activity.

Name _____

Number Roundup

Follow your teacher's directions for the roundup.
Record your score after each turn.

Number	Rounded to	I rounded up (+1)	down (−1)	Score 10

Bonus Box: Round the year you were born to the nearest tens, hundreds, and thousands places.

How To Extend The Lesson:

- Program several new sets of index cards (or use copies of the pattern below) for the Number Roundup. Place a set of the cards and several blank copies of page 49 in a learning center for student pairs to use.

- Create a daily rounding problem for students to solve at the beginning of each math lesson. For example, challenge students to use the numerals 4, 3, 6, and 8 to write a number that would be rounded to 4,000.

- Place students in pairs for a rounding reinforcement activity. Have each student take a turn rolling a die four times, writing down in order the number shown on each roll. Have the student round the resulting number to the nearest thousand. Instruct the pair to repeat the activity until each partner has rounded ten numbers.

- Reinforce rounding practice with a jar of pennies. Have each student select five pennies and round the date on each coin to the nearest tens, hundreds, and thousands places.

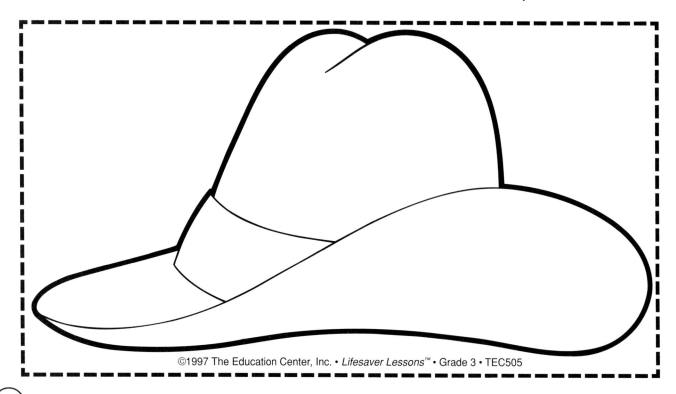

©1997 The Education Center, Inc. • *Lifesaver Lessons™* • Grade 3 • TEC505

Calculation Carnival

Sharpen estimation skills and review basic math concepts with this cooperative-group activity.

Skill: Estimating; practicing number order, place value, subtraction

Estimated Lesson Time: 45 minutes

Teacher Preparation:

1. Duplicate page 53 for each student.
2. Fill four transparent containers with varied amounts of small objects (dried beans, marbles, dry cereal, math counters).
3. Place each of the containers at a separate numbered station that small groups will visit.

Materials:

1 copy of page 53 per student
4 transparent containers, such as glass jars or plastic cups
4 kinds of small objects to place in the containers (varied amount in each container)
4 labels for stations

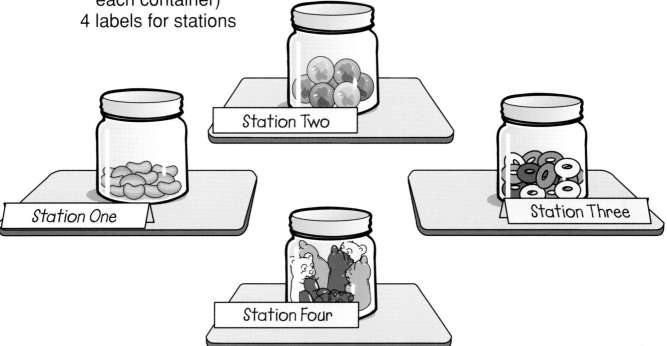

Station One
Station Two
Station Three
Station Four

Estimating and practicing number order, place value, subtraction (51)

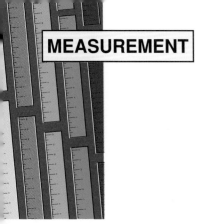
Introducing The Lesson:

Ask students if they have ever been to a carnival. Have students list things they might see at a carnival. Tell them that when you go to a carnival, you like to watch the person at the guessing booth. Ask students if they think they would be good estimators. Hold up one of the transparent containers of objects and ask students to estimate how many objects are in the container. Then ask them to take part in a Calculation Carnival.

Steps:

1. Tell students that they will be working in cooperative groups to estimate the number of objects in the container at each station. After they have made their estimates, each group will complete the rest of the problem-solving activities before moving to the next station.

2. Distribute a copy of page 53 to each student. Divide your class into four cooperative groups, and assign each group to a station for its starting point.

3. Allow time for each group to complete the activities at the first station; then have each group move to the next station in numerical order. Continue in the same fashion until each group has completed all four stations.

4. Challenge each group to complete the Bonus Box activity.

An estimate is a guess at a number. If someone asks you how long it will take you to do your homework and you say, "About an hour," you have made an estimate.

Name _____

Calculation Carnival

At each station, first estimate the number of objects in the container.
Record your estimate.
Then complete the information for that station.

Station One
- My estimate: _____
- Other estimates in my group: _____ _____ _____ _____ _____ _____
- My group's estimates from least to greatest:

  _____ _____ _____ _____ _____ _____ _____
- The actual number of objects: _____
- The difference between my estimate and the actual number: _____
- The actual number has _____ hundreds, _____ tens, and _____ ones.

Station Two
- My estimate: _____
- Other estimates in my group: _____ _____ _____ _____ _____ _____
- My group's estimates from least to greatest:

  _____ _____ _____ _____ _____ _____ _____
- The actual number of objects: _____
- The difference between my estimate and the actual number: _____
- The actual number has _____ hundreds, _____ tens, and _____ ones.

Station Three
- My estimate: _____
- Other estimates in my group: _____ _____ _____ _____ _____ _____
- My group's estimates from least to greatest:

  _____ _____ _____ _____ _____ _____ _____
- The actual number of objects: _____
- The difference between my estimate and the actual number: _____
- The actual number has _____ hundreds, _____ tens, and _____ ones.

Station Four
- My estimate: _____
- Other estimates in my group: _____ _____ _____ _____ _____ _____
- My group's estimates from least to greatest:

  _____ _____ _____ _____ _____ _____ _____
- The actual number of objects: _____
- The difference between my estimate and the actual number: _____
- The actual number has _____ hundreds, _____ tens, and _____ ones.

Bonus Box: Find the difference between the greatest and least estimate at each station. Write the difference by the group's least-to-greatest information and circle it.

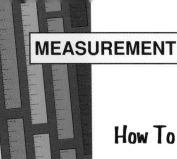
How To Extend The Lesson:

- Use this activity once a week to reinforce estimation skills. Ask students to take turns bringing in small objects to fill the containers.

- Set up a jelly-bean jar. Have each student write his estimate of the number of jelly beans in the jar on a copy of the pattern below. Award the jar to the student with the closest estimation.

- Give each student a small paper cup. Have each student estimate how many pieces of popcorn will fill his cup. Provide popped popcorn, and have each student count the pieces as he fills his cup to check his estimate. Then let students eat the results.

- Expand the numbered stations to include weights. Place a scale at each station and have the group weigh the objects in the container.

- Designate an Estimation Celebration Day. Include appropriate activities throughout the day, such as estimating the number of steps it takes to cross the classroom, the length of a desktop, the height of five math books in a stack, the number of times a student can write his name in one minute, and the number of crackers in a package. Have each student make his estimate, record it on paper, and then complete the activity. Compare the estimates to the actual results.

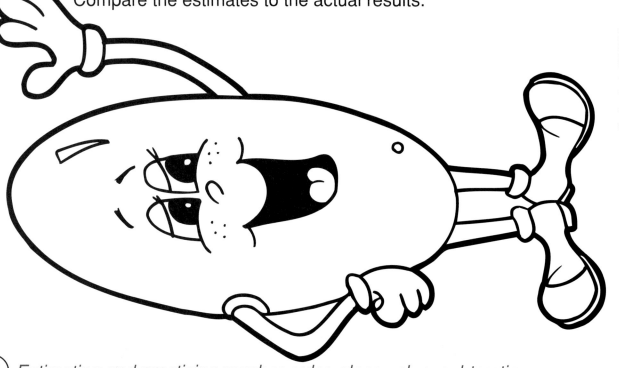

©1997 The Education Center, Inc. • *Lifesaver Lessons*™ • Grade 3 • TEC505

Measurement Quest

Challenge your class to use both standard and metric units of linear measurement.

Skill: Using linear measurement

Estimated Lesson Time: 45 minutes

Teacher Preparation:
1. Duplicate page 57 for each student.
2. Gather the materials listed below.

Materials:
1 copy of page 57 per student
1 ruler with both standard and metric units per student (or use the pattern on page 56 to duplicate a class supply)
objects in desks and in the classroom

Teacher Reference:
Ways To Measure Without A Ruler
• a quarter is about 1" wide
• a dollar bill is about 6" long
• many floor tiles are 12" square
• the tip of your pinkie finger is about 1 cm wide
• a nickel is about 2 cm wide

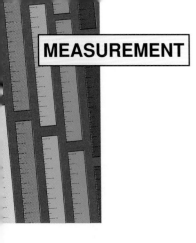

Introducing The Lesson:

Tell students to get ready for a measurement adventure! Ask each of them to look in his desk and find an object about one inch in length. Compare the objects that students have identified.

Steps:

1. Supply each student with a ruler. Ask students to look at the one-inch mark and measure the objects they chose.

2. Tell students that they are going on a measurement search. They will each have a list of lengths and will find an object that is the length of each measurement on the list.

3. Distribute a copy of page 57 to each student.

4. Challenge students to complete the Bonus Box activity.

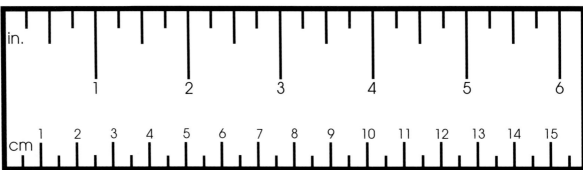

©1997 The Education Center, Inc. • *Lifesaver Lessons*™ • Grade 3 • TEC505

Name_____ *Linear measurement*

Measurement Quest

Use your ruler to draw a line for each of the lengths below.
Find an object in the classroom to match each length.
Write the name of the object above the line you have drawn.

1. 1 inch

2. 4 inches

3. 3 centimeters

4. 6 inches

5. 8 centimeters

6. 2 inches

7. 12 centimeters

8. 7 centimeters

9. 5 inches

10. 15 centimeters

Bonus Box: Measure five items in your desk using both inches and centimeters. Record the items and their lengths on the back of this page.

57

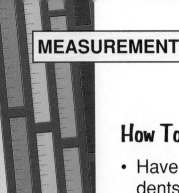

How To Extend The Lesson:

• Have each student create a line drawing with his ruler. Challenge students to include lines ranging from 1 centimeter to 15 centimeters in length.

• Use linear measurement for practice in following directions. Have students listen to your instructions to draw a line three inches long, a box five centimeters square, and other lines and figures.

• Give each student a copy of the form below. Ask students to write their spelling words, then measure the words to see how long they are in inches and in centimeters.

• Supply students with edible manipulatives such as graham crackers, pretzel sticks, or dry cereal. Have students measure them and record the length and width information before eating the treats.

• Create a nonstandard unit of measurement such as the paper clip or an unused crayon length. Have students measure several objects with the new unit and record their lengths and widths.

Spelling word	Length in	
	inches	centimeters
1.		
2.		
3.		
4.		
5.		
6.		
7.		
8.		
9.		
10.		

Terrific Temperatures

Reinforce thermometer skills with temperatures from around the globe.

Skill: Reading a thermometer

Estimated Lesson Time: 30 minutes

Teacher Preparation:

1. Duplicate page 61 for each student.
2. Make an overhead transparency from the pattern on page 60.

Materials:

1 copy of page 61 per student
1 overhead transparency

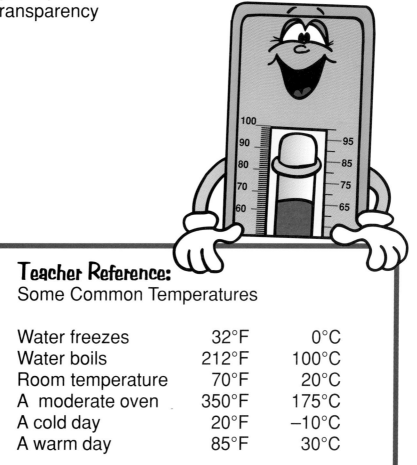

Teacher Reference:

Some Common Temperatures

Water freezes	32°F	0°C
Water boils	212°F	100°C
Room temperature	70°F	20°C
A moderate oven	350°F	175°C
A cold day	20°F	−10°C
A warm day	85°F	30°C

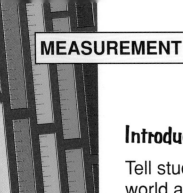

Introducing The Lesson:

Tell students that they will be looking at temperatures from around the world as they practice recording data on a thermometer. Inform students that they will be looking at average temperatures from the month of January. Ask students to name some average winter temperatures for your region.

Steps:

1. Show students an overhead transparency of the thermometer on the bottom of this page. Point out the two-degree increments between each number. Use a wipe-off marker to show students how to record a temperature on the thermometer.

2. Have students practice recording some local winter temperatures on the transparency.

3. Distribute a copy of page 61 to each student. Provide time for students to complete the reproducible.

4. Challenge students to complete the Bonus Box activity.

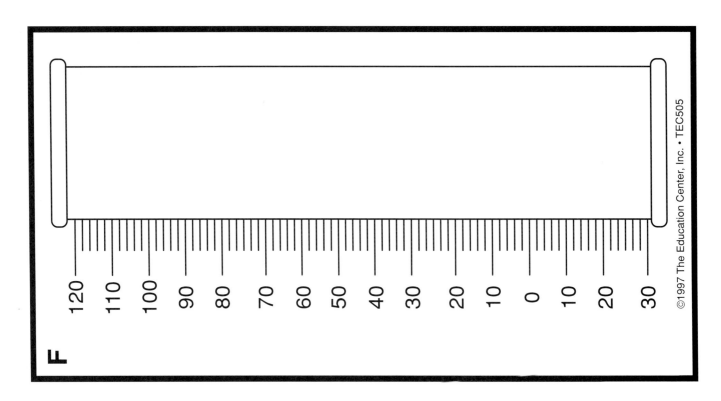

©1997 The Education Center, Inc. • TEC505

Name_____

Terrific Temperatures

Read the sentence below each thermometer.
Find the information on the chart.
Then record each temperature in the blank and on the thermometer.

Station	January Average Daily Temperatures	
	High	Low
Athens, Greece	54	42
Berlin, Germany	35	26
Bombay, India	88	62
Capetown, South Africa	78	60
Copenhagen, Denmark	36	29
Hong Kong, China	64	56
Lima, Peru	82	66
Oslo, Norway	30	20

1.

The high temperature for Oslo, Norway, is _____°F.

2.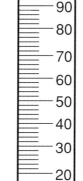

The low temperature for Lima, Peru, is _____°F.

3.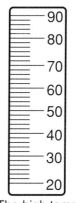

The high temperature for Copenhagen, Denmark, is _____°F.

4.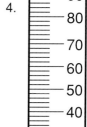

The low temperature for Athens, Greece, is _____°F.

5.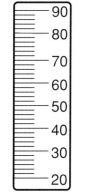

The high temperature for Capetown, South Africa, is _____°F.

6.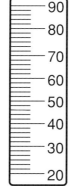

The low temperature for Bombay, India, is _____°F.

7.

The low temperature for Berlin, Germany, is _____°F.

8.

The low temperature for Hong Kong, China, is _____°F.

Bonus Box: On another sheet of paper, draw a thermometer showing your favorite temperature.

61

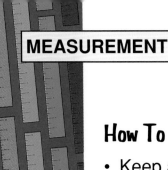

How To Extend The Lesson:

• Keep a daily record of the high temperature. Have a student volunteer show the temperature each day on an enlarged, laminated copy of the thermometer pattern on page 60.

• Have students research to find the average monthly high and low temperatures for your region. Then have students use the data to find out which month has the coldest temperatures, the warmest temperatures, the greatest amount of difference in temperature, and the least amount of difference in temperature.

• Discuss with your students the effect temperature has on the plants and animals of a region. Have students research to find which plants and animals prefer warmer climates and which prefer colder climates.

• Have students keep a record of the low temperatures for a week. Then have students use the information to create a class line graph. For an added challenge, ask students to also record the high temperatures and add the information to the graph with a different color.

• Share the following temperature-related literature with your students:
   —*Fifty Below Zero* by Robert Munsch (Annick Press, 1986)
   —*The Science Book Of Hot & Cold* by Neil Ardley (Harcourt Brace Juvenile Books, 1992)
   —*Temperature* by Brenda Walpole (Gareth Stevens, Inc.; 1995)
   —*Weather Forecasting* by Gail Gibbons (Simon & Schuster Children's Books, 1993)

Our Favorite Things

From raindrops on roses to whiskers on kittens, students will make dazzling discoveries as they graph a collection of class favorites.

Skill: Creating a bar graph

Estimated Lesson Time: 40 minutes

Teacher Preparation:
1. Duplicate page 65 for each student.
2. Provide a bag of jelly beans or other multicolored candy. Each student will need one piece of candy (but have extras so each student will not be limited when choosing his favorite color).

Materials:
1 copy of page 65 per student
1 bag of jelly beans or another candy (1 candy
    per student plus extras)
crayons

Teacher Reference:
A Dozen Things To Graph

How many…
- people are in your family?
- pets do you own?
- buttons do you have on?
- cousins do you have?
- letters are in your name?
- trees are in your yard?
- pockets are you wearing?

What's your favorite…
- TV show?
- sandwich?
- sport?
- song?
- planet?

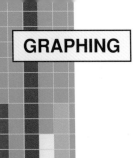

Introducing The Lesson:

Tell your students that this lesson will show their favorites! Hold up the bag of jelly beans or other colored candies. Ask each student to select one piece of his favorite color of candy.

Steps:

1. Tell students that you notice many different favorites. Explain that a good way to record information about students' favorites is to create a graph. Ask students to identify their favorites from such topics as ice-cream flavors, cartoon shows, and sports.

2. Write each of three topic titles on the board. Have each student name his favorite under each topic as you record his responses on the board.

3. Distribute a copy of page 65 to each student.

4. Divide students into three groups and assign each group a topic from the board to graph. Have each group complete page 65 together.

5. Challenge students to complete the Bonus Box activity.

ice-cream flavors	cartoon shows	sports
I mint chocolate chip	III Rocket Ranger	III football
III cookies-'n'-cream	IIII Detective Dawg	IIII basketball
IIII rocky road	III Rags Rabbit	IIII soccer
II cherry vanilla	III Silly Squid	II baseball
IIII strawberry	II Farmer Fox	II tennis

Creating a bar graph

Name _____ *Graphing*

Our Favorite Things

Write the name of the topic as the title of your
  graph.
Write one of the favorites from the board below
  each column.
Color the graph to show which choices are favorites in
  your class.

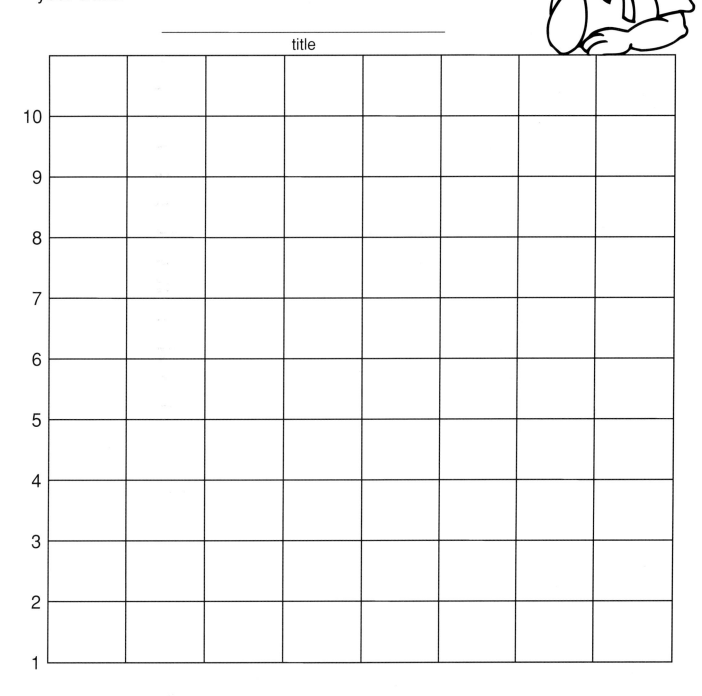

_____
title

10
9
8
7
6
5
4
3
2
1

___ ___ ___ ___ ___ ___

Bonus Box: On the back of this paper, draw a picture to show which choice had the most
boxes colored in.

©1997 The Education Center, Inc. • *Lifesaver Lessons™* • Grade 3 • TEC505

65

How To Extend The Lesson:

- After reading a story, have each student decide on her favorite character. Have the class make graphs to show the results.

- On each Friday, ask students to choose which cafeteria lunch was their favorite that week. Have students graph the results.

- Ask each student to wear a shirt of her favorite color to school on a certain day. Make a human graph by having students stand in lines according to their shirt colors.

- Have each student take a copy of page 65 home and make a graph of items in his favorite room of his house. If desired, help students program the columns with common items—such as chairs, tables, beds, windows, and lamps—or send home a note asking a parent to help the child program this graph. Have students bring the resulting graphs back to school and share the information.

- As each student completes an extension activity, reward her with a copy of the award pattern below.

The results are in...
and when it comes to graphing, You're GREAT!

To:_____ From:_____

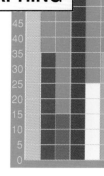

Cat, Dog, Fish, Frog...
What's The Most Popular Pet?

Conduct a class survey to determine the favorite type of pet; then have your students graph the results.

Skill: Creating a line graph

Estimated Lesson Time: 40 minutes

Teacher Preparation:
1. Duplicate the reproducible on page 69 for each student.
2. Provide a sheet of paper for each student to use as a tally sheet, or duplicate a class supply of the tally sheet on page 70.

Materials:
1 copy of page 69 per student
1 sheet of paper or tally sheet per student

Teacher Reference:
Questions To Follow Up A Graphing Activity
1. Which column had the most?
2. Which column had the least?
3. How many more are in column ___ than in column ___?
4. What is the total of column ___ and column ___?
5. Are any columns the same?
6. Which two columns have the greatest difference?
7. How many total responses were there?
8. What statements could be made using the results of the graph?

Introducing The Lesson:

Tell your students that they will gather information to find out which type of pet is most popular with their classmates. After gathering the information, each student will record the results on a line graph.

Steps:

1. Distribute a sheet of paper or a copy of the tally sheet to each student. Show students how to list each category and how to record a tally mark for each response.

2. Have each student stand and name the type of pet(s) she has at home. Assist students in making tally marks in the correct place on their tally sheets as each response is made. As different types of pets are named, it may be necessary for students to list new categories.

3. After each student has had a turn, ask the class to total the tally marks for each category on their tally sheets.

4. Distribute a copy of page 69 to each student. Show the students how to set up categories for the graph to match the information on their tally sheets.

5. Show students how to transfer the information from their tally sheets to the line graph by placing a dot on the appropriate line.

6. After students have completed their graphs, challenge them to complete the Bonus Box activity.

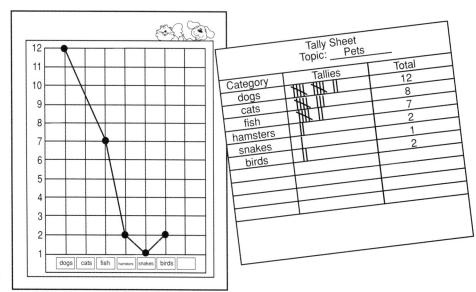

Creating a line graph

Cat, Dog, Fish, Frog…What's The Most Popular Pet?

Use the results of your tally sheet to construct a line graph.

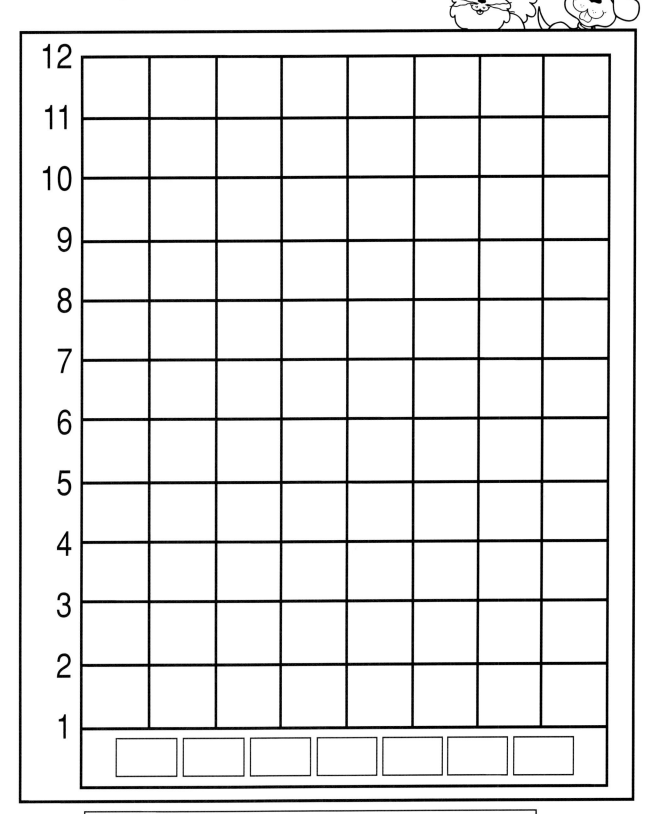

Bonus Box: On another sheet of paper, tell which pet is most popular. Then list three reasons why it is a popular pet.

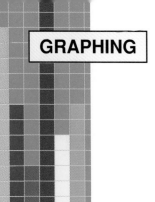

How To Extend The Lesson:

- Have each student conduct another survey with the tally sheet, then graph the results on a copy of the line-graph form. Students can survey to find out the class's favorite color, day of the week, holiday, or type of pizza; or students may wish to create their own survey questions.

- Reinforce comparison skills by having students work in pairs to survey different classrooms. Decide on a question for the survey. Assign each student pair a classroom to interview. Have the pair record the results on a line graph. Then post the completed line graphs and ask students to compare the findings.

- Place students in groups of four. Give each group a bag of colored candies or fruit snacks. Ask each group to sort the different flavors in the bag, then record the results on a line graph. After graphing the results, invite each group to equally divide the pieces and enjoy a snack!

Tally Sheet
Topic:_____

Category	Tallies	Total

Incredible, Edible Circle Graphs

*Have your students create and compare circle graphs.
Then eat the results!*

Skill: Creating a circle graph

Estimated Lesson Time: 30 minutes

Teacher Preparation:
1. Duplicate the reproducible on page 73 for each student.
2. Provide a brown, paper lunch bag for each group of four students.
3. Place a cup of colored, fruit-flavored cereal pieces (such as Froot Loops®) in each bag.

Materials:
1 copy of page 73 per student
1 brown, paper lunch bag for each group
colored, fruit-flavored cereal
crayons

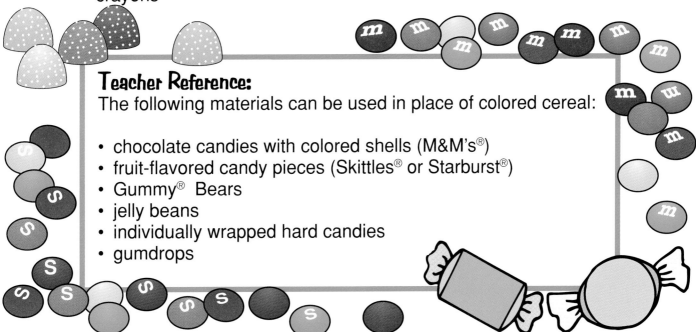

Teacher Reference:
The following materials can be used in place of colored cereal:

- chocolate candies with colored shells (M&M's®)
- fruit-flavored candy pieces (Skittles® or Starburst®)
- Gummy® Bears
- jelly beans
- individually wrapped hard candies
- gumdrops

Introducing The Lesson:

Tell your students that they will be constructing a special graph to record information about a tasty topic. Students will work in groups to gather information, record data, and compare results about fruit-flavored cereal pieces.

Steps:

1. Distribute a copy of page 73 to each student.

2. Place students in groups of four. Provide each group with an assortment of crayons and a brown, paper lunch sack containing a cup of fruit-flavored cereal pieces.

3. Instruct each group member to reach into the bag without looking and select eight pieces of cereal. Have her arrange the pieces on the appropriate section of the reproducible, placing like colors side by side.

4. After each child has had a turn, have students color the graphs to show the results of each group member.

5. Instruct students to write a statement under each graph.

6. Challenge students to complete the Bonus Box activity.

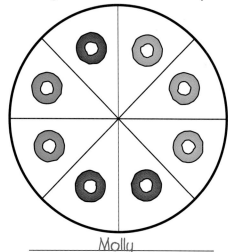

Molly
My name:
A statement about the graph:
There are the same amount
of red and blue pieces.

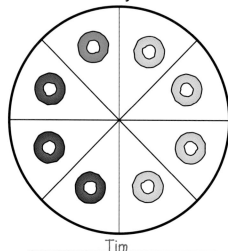

Tim
My name:
A statement about the graph:
There are more yellow
pieces than any other color.

Creating a circle graph

Incredible, Edible Circle Graphs

Follow your teacher's directions to complete the graphs below.

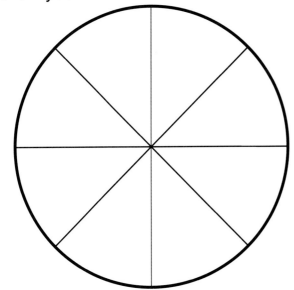

My name: _____
A statement about the graph:
_____

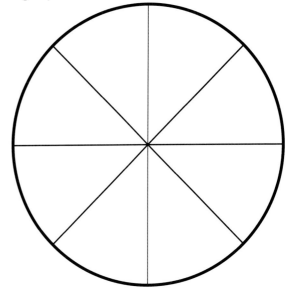

Group member's name: _____
A statement about the graph:
_____

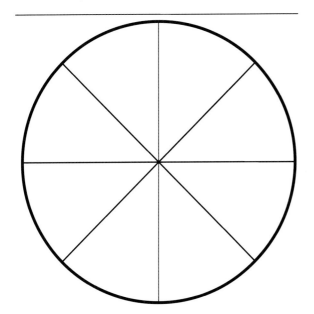

Group member's name: _____
A statement about the graph:
_____

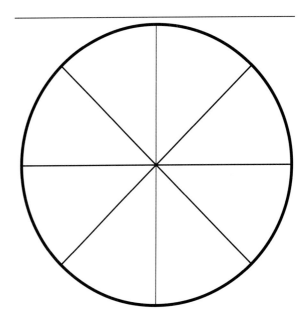

Group member's name: _____
A statement about the graph:
_____

Bonus Box: On another sheet of paper, tell which colors were picked most often and least often. Then write two other conclusions about the graphs.

73

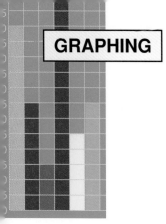
How To Extend The Lesson:

• Provide each group with another copy of the reproducible and a penny. Instruct each student to flip the coin eight times and record the number of heads and tails on a circle graph. After each group member has had a turn, have the students compare the results.

• Reinforce fractional numbers as you discuss the graphs. Have each student make a statement about the graph using fractions to describe the results.

• Distribute a copy of the ten-section circle graph below to each student. Instruct each student to think of a survey topic, such as favorite colors, to chart on the graph. Provide time for students to collect data from their classmates, then show the results on their graphs.

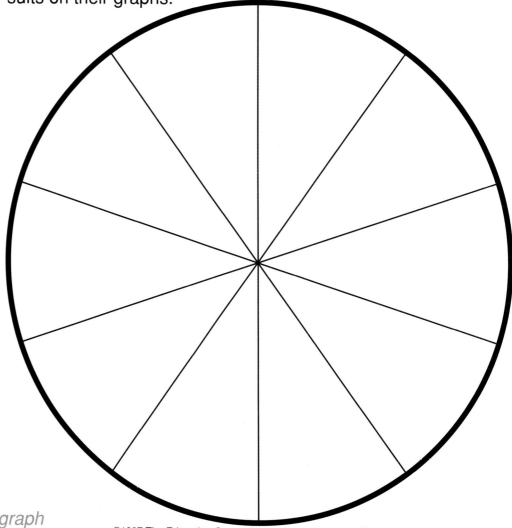

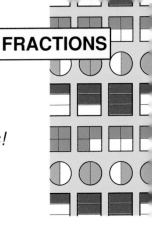

Fraction Sale
Check out these bargain prices for practice in working with fractions!

Skill: Recognizing the fractions of 1/2, 1/3, and 1/4

Estimated Lesson Time: 30 minutes

Teacher Preparation:
Duplicate page 77 for each student.

Materials:
1 copy of page 77 per student

Quick Tip:
Help students remember which number is the numerator and which is the denominator with this reminder:

The **n**umerator is **n**orth of the line.

The **d**enominator is **d**own below the line.

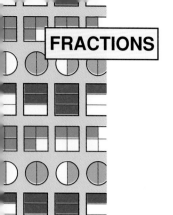

Introducing The Lesson:

Tell students that they are going to practice shopping for bargains with the help of fractions. To demonstrate how to determine a sale price, draw a price tag showing $12 and 12 one-dollar bills below it on the board as shown below. Then tell students that the cost of the item has been marked down. The sale price is one-fourth off the original price. Model the following steps for determining the sale price.

Steps:

1. Group the dollar bills in four equal parts. Explain that each group represents 1/4 of the total amount.

2. Since the sale is for one-fourth off the original amount, cross out one of the groups. Explain that one-fourth of the price has been deducted.

3. Count the remaining dollar bills. Explain that the sale price is the amount left after one-fourth of the total cost was deducted.

4. Repeat the procedure, having students determine the sale price with a discount of one-half and one-third of the $12.

5. Distribute a copy of page 77 to each student. Provide time for students to complete the reproducible.

6. Challenge students to complete the Bonus Box activity.

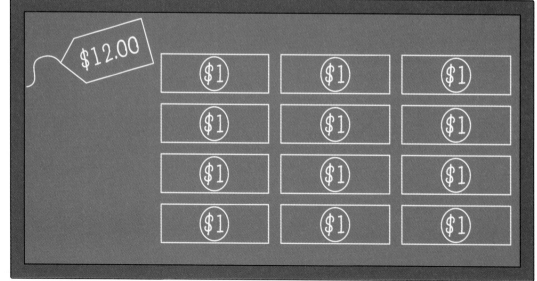

Recognizing the fractions of 1/2, 1/3, and 1/4

Fraction Sale

Find out the price of each item at the sporting goods sale.

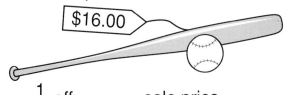

$16.00

$\frac{1}{2}$ off = _____   sale price = _____

$\frac{1}{4}$ off = _____

sale price = _____

$8.00

$\frac{1}{4}$ off = _____

sale price = _____

$12.00

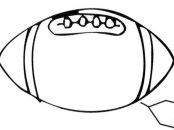

$\frac{1}{3}$ off = _____

sale price = _____

$9.00

$10.00

$\frac{1}{2}$ off = _____

sale price = _____

$15.00

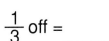

$\frac{1}{3}$ off = _____

sale price = _____

Bonus Box: How much money would you save if you bought every item on sale?

©1997 The Education Center, Inc. • *Lifesaver Lessons*™ • Grade 3 • TEC505 • Key p. 95

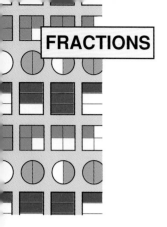

How To Extend The Lesson:

- Give each student an 8" x 8" piece of paper. Have each student fold the paper in half and use a black crayon to visually divide the paper on the fold. Instruct each student to decorate each half of the paper with colored markers or crayons. Glue the completed squares to a butcher-paper backing to create a fraction quilt. Repeat the activity, having students fold their papers into thirds and into fourths.

- Select 12 student volunteers to come to the front of the room. Ask them to arrange themselves in fractional groups, first by fourths, then thirds, and then halves. Repeat the activity with different numbers of student volunteers.

- Have each student draw a picture of a sale item. Instruct the student to include a price tag and the fractional amount that will be deducted. Place the drawings in a learning center with a supply of dollar bills made with the pattern below. Provide time for students to "shop" at the center and determine the sale prices of a specified number of items.

Pattern

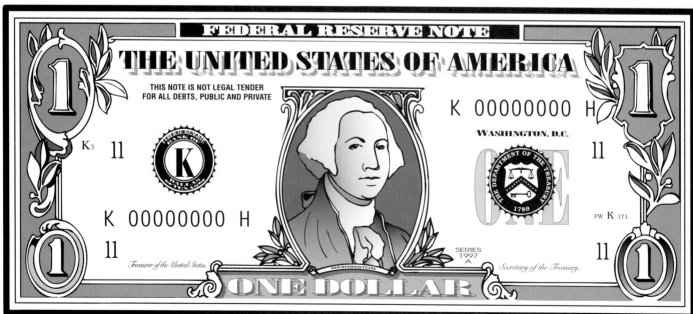

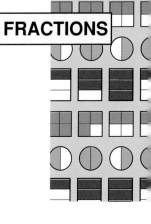

Freewheeling Fractions

*Students will be on a roll with fractions
as they match equivalent amounts!*

Skill: Recognizing equivalent fractions

Estimated Lesson Time: 30 minutes

Teacher Preparation:
1. Duplicate page 81 for each student.
2. Make an overhead transparency of the fraction circles on page 93. Cut out each circle, but do not cut the fractional pieces apart.

Materials:
1 copy of page 81 per student
overhead transparency circles
wipe-off markers
crayons

Teacher Reference:

Share these fraction-related books with your students:
—*Eating Fractions* by Bruce McMillan (Scholastic Inc., 1991)
—*Fraction Action* by Loreen Leedy (Holiday House, Inc.; 1996)
—*Fraction Fun* by David Adler (Holiday House, Inc.; 1996)
—*How Many Ways Can You Cut A Pie?* by Jane Moncure (Child's World, 1987)
—*How Pizza Came To Queens* by Dayal K. Khalsa (Crown Books For Young Readers, 1989)

Recognizing equivalent fractions (79)

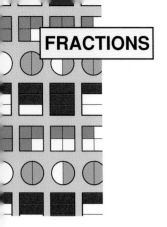

Introducing The Lesson:

Ask students this riddle: What looks like one-half, is worth the same as one-half, but is not called one-half? The answer is two-fourths! Demonstrate this concept to your students by coloring in two-fourths of a fraction-circle transparency and placing it on top of the fraction circle divided into halves. Show students that both fractions name the same amount.

Steps:

1. Tell students that they will be learning different ways to express equivalent fractional amounts. Demonstrate several equivalent fractions by shading in like amounts of the fraction-circle transparencies with a wipe-off marker.

2. Distribute a copy of page 81 to each student. Provide time for students to color the fraction circles to show equivalent amounts.

3. Challenge students to complete the Bonus Box activity.

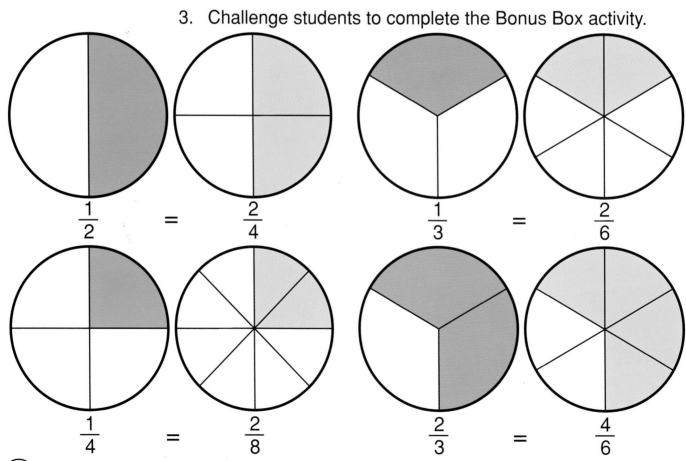

$$\frac{1}{2} = \frac{2}{4} \qquad \frac{1}{3} = \frac{2}{6}$$

$$\frac{1}{4} = \frac{2}{8} \qquad \frac{2}{3} = \frac{4}{6}$$

Name_____

Freewheeling Fractions

Color the wheels on each vehicle to show equivalent fractions.
Then write the equivalent fractional amount.

1. $\dfrac{1}{2} = \dfrac{}{4}$

2. $\dfrac{1}{4} = \dfrac{}{8}$

3. $\dfrac{1}{3} = \dfrac{}{6}$

4. $\dfrac{1}{2} = \dfrac{}{6}$

5. $\dfrac{1}{2} = \dfrac{}{8}$

6. $\dfrac{2}{4} = \dfrac{}{8}$

7. $\dfrac{2}{3} = \dfrac{}{6}$

8. $\dfrac{3}{4} = \dfrac{}{8}$

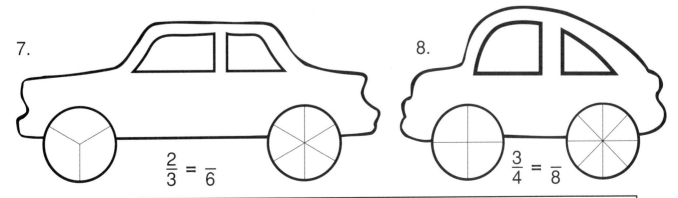

Bonus Box: On another sheet of paper, draw a pizza. Divide it so that eight people would each get one equal slice.

81

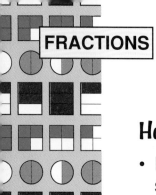

How To Extend The Lesson:

- Provide each student with a ball of clay and a plastic knife. Have each student flatten the ball into a circle, then use the knife to divide it into fractional amounts. Have students compare sizes to determine which fractional pieces are smaller, larger, or equal to each other.

- Play a fraction-recognition game with your students. To prepare for the game, make a spinner from the pattern below. Provide each student with a copy of the fractional circles on page 93. Instruct each student to label the pieces of the circles with their fractional amounts before cutting the circles apart. (If desired, have students color each circle a designated color to help with recognition.)

Play the game as follows:

1. Instruct each student to place the whole circle on his desk.
2. Call out a fraction as determined by the spinner.
3. Each student finds a corresponding piece from his fraction pieces and places it on top of the whole circle.
4. Repeat the process, having students try to cover their circles with the fractional pieces determined by each spin.
5. Players get a point by calling "Trade up!" when two or more pieces can be exchanged for a larger one. Each time a point is earned, make a tally mark on the board.
6. Play until all equivalences have been "traded up" and each student's circle has been covered with two halves. (Note: If the amount of space left to be covered in the circle is smaller than the fraction called, players must wait until the correct fraction is called.)
7. Add up the points. Challenge students to continue play until ten points have been earned.

Recognizing equivalent fractions   ©1997 The Education Center, Inc. •
Lifesaver Lessons™ • Grade 3 • TEC505

Wally's Watch

Students will use time-telling skills to answer these problems like clockwork!

Skill: Telling time to the quarter hour

Estimated Lesson Time: 30 minutes

Teacher Preparation:
1. Duplicate the reproducible on page 85 for each student.
2. Gather a supply of face-clock manipulatives, or make copies of the patterns on page 94.

Materials:
1 copy of page 85 per student
1 clock manipulative per student

Teacher Reference:
Discuss these timely sayings with your students:

- Time flies.
- In the nick of time
- A stitch in time saves nine.
- The time of your life
- Time out
- Time is money.
- In the right place at the wrong time
- Wasting time
- For the time being
- Time's on your side.

Introducing The Lesson:

Tell students that your friend Wally the Moose is always early for everything because his watch is 15 minutes fast. Explain that if it is really 12:00, Wally's watch will read 12:15. Use a manipulative face clock to show 12:00; then demonstrate how to count by fives to 15 while moving the minute hand ahead 15 minutes. Tell students that they will practice determining what time Wally's watch will read.

Steps:

1. Distribute a manipulative clock to each student. Instruct each student to position the hands so that the clock reads 12:00. Then count together as everyone moves the minute hand so that the clock reads 12:15.

2. Have students continue guided practice. Announce a starting time for the clocks, and have students determine what Wally's watch would read by moving the minute hand 15 minutes ahead. Continue with several examples until students have understanding.

3. Distribute a copy of page 85 to each student. Provide time for students to complete the reproducible.

4. Challenge students to complete the Bonus Box activity.

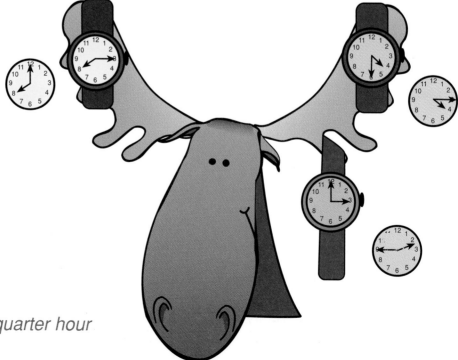

Name_____

Wally's Watch

Wally's watch is set 15 minutes fast.
Look at the clock that shows the real time.
Write the real time, and then tell what time Wally's watch
would show.

Example:
The real time is __3:00__ .
Wally's watch would show ____3:15____ .

1.  Time to call
Mama Moose!

The real time is _____ .
Wally's watch would show _____ .

5.  Remember to watch
"Moose On The
Loose."

The real time is _____ .
Wally's watch would show _____ .

2. Meet Morris
for a movie.

The real time is _____ .
Wally's watch would show _____ .

6.  Don't forget the
wildlife tour!

The real time is _____ .
Wally's watch would show _____ .

3. Brush teeth and get
ready for bed.

The real time is _____ .
Wally's watch would show _____ .

7.  Appointment to
polish antlers.

The real time is _____ .
Wally's watch would show _____ .

4.  Moose Scouts
meeting!

The real time is _____ .
Wally's watch would show _____ .

8.  Time to get a
new watch!

The real time is _____ .
Wally's watch would show _____ .

Bonus Box: Tell what time Wally's watch would show when school starts, when you go to lunch, and when school is over.

85

©1997 The Education Center, Inc. • *Lifesaver Lessons*™ • Grade 3 • TEC505 • Key p. 95

How To Extend The Lesson:

• Make a class clock with your students. Have 12 students sit in a circle to represent the numbers on a clock face. Place one student in the middle of the circle and give her two sentence strips—a long one to represent the minute hand, and a shorter one to represent the hour hand. Call out times to the quarter hour and have students position the hands to show the times.

• Throughout the day, assign students various tasks that will take 15 minutes to complete. At the beginning of each activity, instruct students to write down the starting time and predict what the ending time will be. Then have students read silently, solve a set of math problems, write spelling words, or work on another assignment for 15 minutes. When time is up, have students write down the ending time and compare it to their predictions.

• Use the digital clock pattern below to have students practice reading digital times as well as analog times.

1	00
2	05
3	10
4	15
5	20
6	25
7	30
8	35
9	40
10	45
11	50
12	55

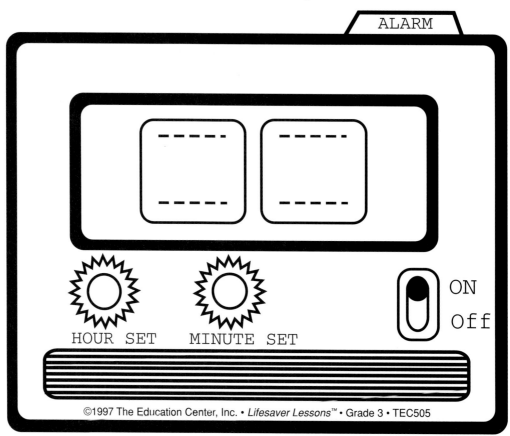

©1997 The Education Center, Inc. • *Lifesaver Lessons*™ • Grade 3 • TEC505

From Time To Time

Provide practice with time-telling skills as students try their hands at creating clock faces.

Skill: Telling time to five minutes

Estimated Lesson Time: 30 minutes

Teacher Preparation:
1. Duplicate a copy of page 89 for each student.
2. Write a different digital time on each of ten index cards.
3. Place the index cards inside a large envelope.
4. Duplicate the clock pattern on page 94, or use a face-clock manipulative.

Materials:
1 copy of page 89 per student
10 programmed index cards
1 large envelope
1 face-clock manipulative

Teacher Reference:
Test your students' concepts of time with these time trivia questions:

- How many hours are in one day?
- How many minutes are in one hour?
- How many seconds are in one minute?
- What hours are A.M. times?
- What hours are P.M. times?
- When is it noon?
- When is it midnight?
- What does the term "half past the hour" mean?
- What does the term "quarter past the hour" mean?
- Which seems longer—an hour of homework, or an hour of free time?

Introducing The Lesson:

Tell students that they are going to use their ability to count by fives to practice telling time. Remind students that each number on the clock represents a five-minute increment. Touch each number on the clock while counting by fives to review with students how to read the minute hand.

Steps:

1. Set the clock manipulative for 1:15. Ask students to identify the hour and minutes shown on the clock.

2. Have students read several other times on the clock for guided practice.

3. Distribute a copy of page 89 to each student. Tell students that you will show them cards with digital times written on them. Each student will draw hands on a clock face to correspond with each card.

4. Select one card at a time from the envelope. Show the card to your students and provide time for them to draw hands corresponding with its digital time.

5. After students have completed the reproducible, challenge them to complete the Bonus Box activity.

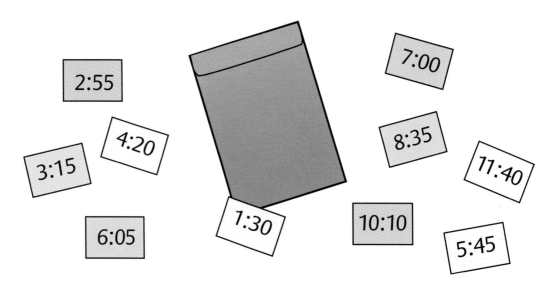

From Time To Time

Draw the hands on each clock face as your teacher shows you a digital time.

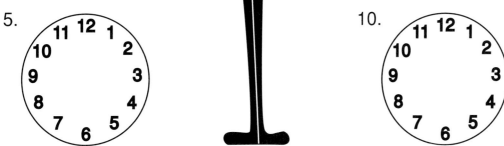

1.

2.

3.

4.

5.

6.

7.

8.

9.

10.

Bonus Box: On the back of this paper, list six things that take about five minutes each to complete.

89

How To Extend The Lesson:

- Repeat the activity after programming another set of index cards. Or, if you prefer, have each student program one index card. Collect the cards and use them with the activity.

- Challenge students to complete the activity in reverse. Put ten pictures of standard clocks in the envelope. Show one clock at a time to your students and have them write the digital time on a sheet of paper.

- Ask students to predict several tasks that they think can be accomplished in five minutes. How many spelling words do they think they can write in five minutes? How many pages could they read? After students have made predictions, try the activities and discuss the results.

- Have students make their own sandglasses to practice time-telling skills. Collect the necessary materials and have each student follow the instructions below for constructing a sandglass.

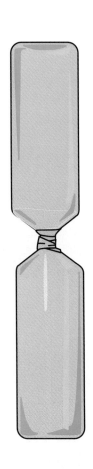

   Materials
   Each student will need:
   2 empty, plastic two-liter bottles—well rinsed and dried
   packing tape
   2 cups of sand
   access to a funnel
   access to a clock with a second hand

   1. Use the funnel to pour the sand into one of the bottles.
   2. Tape the second bottle to the first one as shown.
   3. Look at the second hand of a clock. When the hand reaches the 12, invert the sandglass and determine how long it takes for the sand to pour from one bottle to the other.

- Afterward, ask students to predict how much sand it would take to make a one-minute timer, a two-minute timer, and a five-minute timer. For an added challenge, ask students to think of a way to slow down the flow of sand from one bottle to the other.

Place-Value Patterns

Use with "Regrouping Rally" on page 7 and the second extension activity on page 46.

Coin Patterns

Use with the third extension activity on page 14.

Fraction Circles

Use with "Freewheeling Fractions" on page 79 and the second extension activity on page 82.

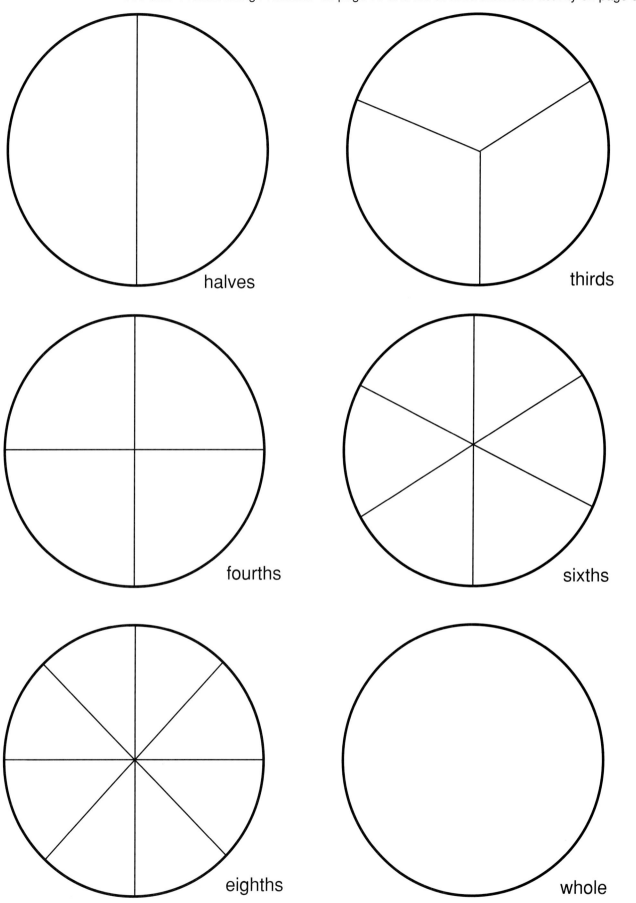

halves

thirds

fourths

sixths

eighths

whole

Analog Clock Pattern
Use with "Wally's Watch" on page 83.

minute hand

hour hand

Answer Key

Page 9
1. 44 (red)
2. 52 (red)
3. 38 (blue)
4. 72 (red)
5. 54 (red)
6. 77 (blue)
7. 56 (red)
8. 40 (red)
9. 69 (blue)
10. 81 (red)
11. 91 (red)
12. 78 (blue)
13. 94 (red)
14. 61 (red)
15. 94 (blue)

Page 13

Joe's Snack Attack

Joe has 90¢.
He bought a sno-cone.
How much money is left?

$$\begin{array}{r} {}^{8\ 1}90 \\ -\ 38 \\ \hline 52¢ \end{array}$$

Then Joe bought some peanuts.
How much money is left?

$$\begin{array}{r} {}^{4\ 1}52 \\ -\ 25 \\ \hline 27¢ \end{array}$$

Joe also bought popcorn.
How much money is left?

$$\begin{array}{r} {}^{1\ 1}27 \\ -\ 19 \\ \hline 8¢ \end{array}$$

What could Joe buy with the money left over?

__hard candy__

Jane's Snack Attack

Jane has 90¢.
She bought cotton candy.
How much money is left?

$$\begin{array}{r} {}^{8\ 1}90 \\ -\ 48 \\ \hline 42¢ \end{array}$$

Then Jane bought a lollipop.
How much money is left?

$$\begin{array}{r} {}^{3\ 1}42 \\ -\ 27 \\ \hline 15¢ \end{array}$$

Jane also bought a pickle.
How much money is left?

$$\begin{array}{r} 15 \\ -\ 12 \\ \hline 3¢ \end{array}$$

What could Jane buy with the money left over?

__nothing__

Page 37
1. add   4 + 2 + 2 = 8
2. subtract   9 − 4 = 5
3. add   5 + 4 + 7 + 3 = 19
4. add   11 + 14 = 25
5. subtract   84 − 79 = 5
6. subtract   9 − 5 = 4
7. subtract   67 − 35 = 32
8. add   4 + 6 + 3 = 13

Page 45
4, 3, 6, 2
largest number—6,432
smallest number—2,346
smallest numeral in tens place—answers will vary, but the 2
    must be in the tens place
largest numeral in hundreds place—answers will vary, but the 6
    must be in the hundreds place

2, 9, 0, 6
largest number—9,620
smallest number—269
smallest numeral in tens place—answers will vary, but the 0
    must be in the tens place
largest numeral in hundreds place—answers will vary, but the 9
    must be in the hundreds place

7, 8, 1, 5
largest number—8,751
smallest number—1,578
smallest numeral in tens place—answers will vary, but the 1
    must be in the tens place
largest numeral in hundreds place—answers will vary, but the 8
    must be in the hundreds place

3, 0, 8, 4
largest number—8,430
smallest number—348
smallest numeral in tens place—answers will vary, but the 0
    must be in the tens place
largest numeral in hundreds place—answers will vary, but the 8
    must be in the hundreds place

2, 5, 1, 7
largest number—7,521
smallest number—1,257
smallest numeral in tens place—answers will vary, but the 1
    must be in the tens place
largest numeral in hundreds place—answers will vary, but the 7
    must be in the hundreds place

Page 61
1. 30°F
2. 66°F
3. 36°F
4. 42°F
5. 78°F
6. 62°F
7. 26°F
8. 56°F

Page 77

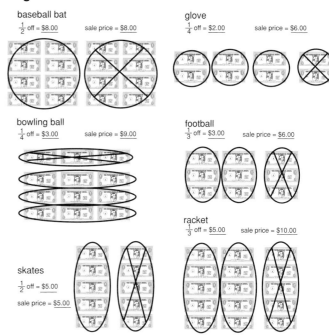

baseball bat
$\frac{1}{2}$ off = $8.00   sale price = $8.00

glove
$\frac{1}{4}$ off = $2.00   sale price = $6.00

bowling ball
$\frac{1}{4}$ off = $3.00   sale price = $9.00

football
$\frac{1}{3}$ off = $3.00   sale price = $6.00

racket
$\frac{1}{3}$ off = $5.00   sale price = $10.00

skates
$\frac{1}{2}$ off = $5.00

sale price = $5.00

Page 81
1. 1/2 = **2**/4
2. 1/4 = **2**/8
3. 1/3 = **2**/6
4. 1/2 = **3**/6
5. 1/2 = **4**/8
6. 2/4 = **4**/8
7. 2/3 = **4**/6
8. 3/4 = **6**/8

Page 85
1. The real time is **2:15**.
   Wally's watch would show **2:30**.

2. The real time is **5:30**.
   Wally's watch would show **5:45**.

3. The real time is **9:00**.
   Wally's watch would show **9:15**.

4. The real time is **7:15**.
   Wally's watch would show **7:30**.

5. The real time is **1:45**.
   Wally's watch would show **2:00**.

6. The real time is **11:30**.
   Wally's watch would show **11:45**.

7. The real time is **10:00**.
   Wally's watch would show: **10:15**.

8. The real time is **4:45**.
   Wally's watch would show **5:00**.

Grade 3 Math Management Checklist

SKILLS	PAGES	DATE(S) USED	COMMENTS
ADDITION & SUBTRACTION			
Basic Facts	3		
Two-Digit Addition With Regrouping	7		
Two-Digit Subtraction With Regrouping	11		
MULTIPLICATION			
Multiplication Facts Through 6	15		
Multiplication Facts Through 10	19		
PROBLEM SOLVING			
Sorting Attributes	23		
Problems With Money	27		
Word Problems	31		
Choosing The Operation	35		
GEOMETRY			
Identifying Shapes	39		
PLACE VALUE			
Place Value To 1,000	43		
Rounding Numerals To Thousands	47		
MEASUREMENT			
Estimation	51		
Linear Measurement	55		
Reading A Thermometer	59		
GRAPHING			
Bar Graphs	63		
Line Graphs	67		
Circle Graphs	71		
FRACTIONS			
Fractions: 1/2, 1/3, 1/4	75		
Equivalent Fractions	79		
TIME			
Time To 1/4 Hour	83		
Time In 5-Minute Increments	87		